C40193940%

BRYLCREAM EASY

BRYLCREAM EASY

True stories from a
rear-gunner, 1939–45

*A tribute to the men of Bomber
Command—of whom I was one*

Donald H. Roberts, DFC

CHIVERS LARGE PRINT
BATH

British Library Cataloguing in Publication Data available

This Large Print edition published by Chivers Press, Bath, 1997.

Published by arrangement with the author.

U.K. Hardcover ISBN 0 7540 3088 1

Photoset, printed and bound in Great Britain by
Redwood Books, Trowbridge, Wiltshire

CONTENTS

*Dedicated to the ground and aircrew squadrons
of Bomber Command*

ACKNOWLEDGMENTS

I wish to gratefully acknowledge the assistance of the following persons and organizations in the production of this book:

Joe Ward, DFM, for his patient and cooperative provision of detailed technical information;

Captain E. Gwyn Williams, CD, Curator and Manager of the Royal Australian Air Force Association Museum, Bull Creek, W.A. for his assistance in photography of the museum's Lancaster exhibit;

My wife Ann, for her forebearance of my moods and her patience in hearing me out.

D.R.

PREFACE

In this collection of stories I have tried in a modest way to immortalize some of the many men I knew during the dark days of 1939–45. They are the men of Bomber Command. These are their stories, told in a way I believe is in character with them. I have also recalled my own fears and hopes, plans and dreams, to portray the thoughts, feelings and dread of the early nineteen-forties when comradeship and the thought of loved ones waiting at home were sometimes all we had to sustain us.

The core of each story is true. I have given each character the fictional domestic life I feel he might have enjoyed to show the other side of the man. I am sure similar characters existed in every squadron of whatever command. I was privileged to serve with Bomber Command, where the trials were great and morale high.

Brylcream *Easy* was the callsign of an actual Lancaster flying out of Wickenby, but personal names, dates, targets and locations have been changed to avoid hurt or embarrassment to surviving comrades or the loved ones of those who 'made their final landing'.

If some old 'fly boys', thinking they recognise themselves or a squadron buddy, smile or shed a tear, as I have in the writing, then I will feel my efforts have not been in vain.

For the younger readers, let them see some of the victims of the madness of 1939–45 and work and pray that their children do not suffer the pain, fear and lop-sided joy of having to fight a war.

Donald H. Roberts, Perth, 1992

CHAPTER ONE

SUMMER 1940

I wiped the blood from my face and blew my nose. Clots of blood soiled my handkerchief. I straightened my tie and faced the two airmen standing in front of me.

'How can I thank you. Those bastards would have tramped me into the ground but for you.'

'Don't mention it. You would have done the same for us, I am sure.'

The tall one smiled. It was he who had spoken. The shorter airman was rubbing his jaw where he had received a blow.

The scene was a side street just off Edgeware Road, London. I had been to The Palace to see Gary Cooper in *The Frontiersman*. He had been my favourite film star for years. My mother liked him too. She and I often went to the flicks together before I joined the RAF.

Foolishly, I suppose, I went into a little pub for a drink before walking the mile or so back to my billet. I should have left as soon as they started to rib me.

'Bloody Brylcream Boys! Where were you at Dunkirk? Eh?'

'Sittin' on their arses wiv the bloody birds at 'ome while us poor bloody infantry was art

1

there fightin' the bloody war for 'em.'

'Yeah. All a bunch of pansies, the bloody lot ov 'em.'

The group of drunken soldiers was standing at the bar across from me. I took my modest half pint of bitter ale across to a seat in the corner.

'Look. 'E don't even drink a man-size drink. Bloody pansy.'

One of the group lurched away from his companions and came across. His heavy boots scraped the floor and kicked a chair away. He leaned over the table and leered into my face. His breath stank of fresh beer and stale tobacco. Yellow teeth grinned at me.

'Bloody pansy, ain't cher.'

Whether it was a question or a statement I never found out. He reached out and took my half-empty glass and poured it over the table. I looked into his bloodshot eyes and felt the spilt beer dripping onto my trousers and into my crutch.

I did not move. The man was obviously spoiling for a fight and I was beginning to feel I could oblige him. That is, until I saw the four others grinning encouragement to their companion.

'Go on, Dobber, hit the cunt.'

I looked at the khaki figure in front of me. I'm pretty handy with my fists. A swift left jab to the nose and a right to the jaw would have settled it there and then. If there had only been

2

him. Or him and a mate. But there were five.

The blowzy-looking barmaid looked on disinterestedly, a cigarette drooping from her lips, a glass of clear liquid, probably gin, in her hand. Her crimson fingernails looked like tropical beetles; her fingers like the claws of a chicken. Why had I come into such a place?

I thought about standing up to leave. The door was ten feet away. My tormentor would have to come around the table to stop me. His friends had twenty feet to travel. And they were drunk. I figured the chances of my making the door and clearing the pub were pretty good.

I looked at the man in front of me. He was tall and muscular. Towering, in fact. His rather gross features looked a trifle mongoloid. Thick, moist lips slathered and drooled. Coarse dark hair nearly fused into his eyebrows.

He was now looking towards his friends. I saw my chance and was on my feet, making for the door. I took a step—to be pulled up sharp by my respirator mask. It had caught the protruding arm of the seat.

The delay was enough to give the giant time to lunge. The blow caught me in the face— right on my unguarded nose, in fact. I staggered under the force of it and recovered enough to ward off the second blow. I picked myself up; my fist shot out and I had the satisfaction of seeing the yellow teeth change to red. I aimed another at his jaw. He collapsed

3

onto a chair and slid to the floor.

At that moment, the roof fell in. I felt a blow on the back of my neck. A searing pain sent lights into my eyes. I turned. A huge hand caught me on the side of the head. I weaved away from the khaki figure intent on killing me. A chair broke. Glass smashed. Then arms grabbed me and I felt the cool evening air.

'Run, for God's sake!'

I ran. I ran for perhaps a hundred yards before being stopped by a restraining arm.

'We can stop now. I think we are clear.'

The three of us stood panting, facing each other. I tasted salt as the blood from my nose ran into my mouth.

'Excuse me.'

I walked to the gutter and spat into the drain. Then I looked at the two airmen.

'Bloody idiots! What had you done to upset them?' It was the tall one who spoke.

'Oh, just the wrong place at the wrong time, I think.'

I was a mess. My shirt and tunic were covered with blood, my trousers torn, my knuckles skinned and my face sore. My neck? Yes. I was a mess. But I was lucky it was not worse. I had a vision of those heavy army boots kicking my head and body.

'Where did you fellows come from, anyway?'

'We had just left two girls at their flat and were walking back to our billets. We were passing the pub when we heard the shindig. I was all for minding my own business but Monty here charged in and I was fool enough to follow. Well, we saw you having the daylight punched out of you and, as it was one against five we thought we'd even things up a bit.'

'I'm damned glad you did. They were making a mess of me in there.'

'Mention it not again, old boy. The matter is closed. Let us lick our wounds and press on. Where to, stranger?'

I looked at my tall companion of only a few minutes. His mode of speech amused me at a time when I needed diversion. I was beginning to feel the pain from my beating.

We introduced ourselves. The taller one was Montrose St. John MacNash, a native of the wilds of Ross Shire. The other was Sinclare Cotton—'You'd best call me Fred. Everyone does in the end. Friends, anyway.'

'But your name is Sinclare?'

'Cotton and thread. Fred. Chaps started calling me that at school. I don't mind, really. So make it Fred. I was born in Ceylon. My father works there for the government.'

I laughed as I introduced myself. 'Don Roberts from Ealing. Nothing very romantic, I'm afraid. My family call me Don. But since I've been in the air force everyone calls me Robbie.'

As we walked we discovered we were all applicants for aircrew training and were

5

billeted in St. John's Wood. It took about half an hour to get there. Lights were out and we were late, so we didn't linger for fear of being caught by the service police.

Next morning we were paraded and marched to Lord's cricket ground. I noticed that Monty and Fred were in a neighbouring flight. We got together during the break from tests and interviews. Monty had hopes of being selected for pilot training. We all did. But I knew my maths was not good enough and knew I'd be selected for something else. Fred was the same.

'If I can't be a pilot I'd rather be a gunner. I want to see what the hell goes on. I don't want to be cooped up in a cubby hole wondering what's happening outside. If some bastard is shooting at me I want to be able to shoot back.' It was a point of view I hadn't considered.

A week later we knew our fate. Monty was rejected for pilot training because of astigmatism. Fred and I because of our maths. We were all accepted for air-gunner training.

*　　　*　　　*

About five hundred cadets packed into the ballroom of an old holiday resort on rows of hard, wooden forms. 'Like chickens in a poultry house,' was how Monty described it.

The lecturer limped onto the stage, leaning on a stout ash walking-stick. A squadron leader, no less. He was middle-aged and had on his chest the ribbons of the Military Cross and several from the 1914–18 war. Above them was an embroidered pilot's brevet of the Royal Flying Corps. On his lapels, the badges of the Medical Branch. Snakes twisted around a staff.

He faced us as we settled down. Then lifted his stick and waved it at us. Up and down. Up and down.

'Some of you young buggers will put your penises where I wouldn't put my walking stick.'

There followed an hour of amusing but instructive directions about what not to do with our sexual appendages, and what to do with them if we forgot his fatherly advice. We filed out chastened but wiser, vowing never to look at a female ever again. The shock of it lasted a week.

We did eight weeks at the initial training wing. Night vision training; aircraft recognition; lectures by the dozen. Posting to gunnery school followed. Sighting. Flying training. Air firing. Combat manoeuvres. The intricacies of the Boulton & Paul and Frazer-Nash gun turrets. Hours in the dome trainer, following a silhouette of a German fighter.

Then the examinations. Monty led the marks, with Fred a close second. I was a more modest fourth. We were all very keen.

'If we've got to be wretched air-gunners,

then by God we may as well be good ones.'
Monty was adamant.

Monty's high marks earned him a commission. Fred, I and the others, sergeants.

But Monty had a problem. It turned out that he was an army deserter.

The battalion commander's wife had been attracted to Monty and he had accepted her charms. To cut a long story short, he was actually caught with his pants down by the Colonel. He had escaped through the window and deserted that night. He joined the RAF next day.

'I'd have joined the Navy, but I can't swim. The French Foreign Legion meant a passport and I was sure the old colonel had every port watched for me. I changed my name from McNess to MacNash so my people would never find out the truth. You see, they are in India. Father has a brigade out there. He's not likely to come home till after the war, so I felt I was safe.

He said it as if his father 'has a car out there.'

'Is that why there's always a mixup with your mail?' Fred's question put my own query into words.

'Yes. I always have to explain to the snotty-nosed orderly corporal that my aged grandmother in India is eccentric and can't remember my name.'

We were almost home by now.

'You see. If I accept a commission the

8

airforce might start inquiries and discover I'm an army deserter.'

I laughed and looked at him.

'For Christ's sake, Monty. What the hell? You're in the airforce now. They won't sack you, and they won't return you in irons to the tender mercies of the old colonel. Chances are, he thrashed his wife for being unfaithful and is damned glad you aren't around to boast of your conquest.'

Monty was silent for a minute.

'You know, I hadn't thought of it like that. I think you may be right.'

*　　　*　　　*

During the dull hours of waiting that most of war is, we spent endless hours discussing the building of a new world. Monty had designed an ideal city.

It was built in a series of circles, starting from a powerhouse deep in the earth. He drew a rough diagram.

'And what about the smoke from the furnaces?' I was sure my question would floor him.

'It won't be a thermal powerhouse. It will be powered by a fuel not yet discovered. One that will revolutionize the power industry. I don't quite know how it will be done yet, but believe me, it will be. The heat will be recycled to warm the city through a central heating system.

9

Everything will be recycled. Sewerage. Garbage. Heat. Everything.'

It sounded most improbable. But then, the whole plan was.

'From the underground power plant a building will rise to house the administrative centre, the radio station and the new visual medium being developed—like radio, but it will show pictures. Every house will have one. You'll see. And there'll be avenues and boulevards, intersected by pedestrian malls.'

Fred and I laughed. 'What about the cars? Where will they go?'

He continued. 'There will be no cars. The motor car will be banned from the city to keep the air clean.'

'We'll have to walk everywhere!'

'Of course not. There will be an underground electric train service to every street and pedestrian walks. Slow tracks for shoppers and fast ones for those in a hurry.'

During the long evenings we would scribble on countless pieces of paper. It was our main source of interest.

*   *   *

We were given two weeks leave at the end of our course. The three of us travelled to London so Monty could buy his officer's uniform. We spent the first week at my place in Ealing, then travelled west and spent another week walking

10

through the Forest of Dean.

The pubs in Coleford, Cinderford and Park End saw a lot of us. One memorable night at a little pub in Lydney we drank a little more than usual. It had been a good day. We had walked for miles and talked a lot. We had eaten and there was a fire in the hearth. The lights were low. We were tired, well fed and relaxed. We knew that in a few days we would be flying. And then, who knows?

'I say. Let us make a pact. If any of us gets the chop, the others—whoever survives—goes to see our people. Agreed?'

It was agreed. We solemnly shook hands and drank to it.

*   *   *

Next week, for us, the war began.

CHAPTER TWO

FIRST BLOOD

RAF station Binbrook was home to Twelve Squadron, RAF Bomber Command. After the huts at Stormy Downs, the centrally heated, brick barrack blocks of Binbrook were luxury. The sergeants' mess seemed a sumptuous palace after the airmans' mess we had been used to. Monty of course, had gone to the officers' mess where he was even more comfortable.

The squadron was equipped with Wellington Mark V's—Wimpy's to us. Beautiful aeroplanes we thought. Our end of the plane boasted a four-gun hydraulic turret and the three of us were impatient to get into the air and prove ourselves. We were replacing gunners who had become casualties but we were too young—or too stupid—to be discouraged by this. I learned different as I got older.

My pilot was a rather toffee-nosed flight lieutenant. He was ex-Cranwell and told me so. Often. At the time I was little interested in his past. It was his future that interested me. Would he survive? And if he did, would I survive with him?

The co-pilot was equally toffee-nosed and claimed a connection with royalty. When I met them I feared for my future, socially at least. I could never see the time when I would enjoy their company, or them mine. It was the thing not to become too friendly with the NCOs in one's crew. Officers were invited to the sergeants' mess but never the other way around.

The navigator was different—a nicer chap altogether. A former school teacher from Bath in Somerset, he shared my love for woodlands and bitter beer. The sort of fellow with his feet on the ground, yet had imagination.

The other two members of my crew were flight sergeants. Senior to me in every way. Both had been flying for some time and had been with the squadron in France, before Dunkirk. I realized later that both were at the end of their tether—what we called flak happy—and the Americans, 'combat fatigue'. They were an experienced pair and a hive of information for new birds like us.

Monty went almost immediately on a gunnery leaders' course. Fred and I missed him enormously. Our skippers made our lives miserable—they insisted on being called 'skipper' or 'captain'. I called mine simply 'pilot'. No more. No less.

*　　　*　　　*

The squadron was involved in a heavy training program when we arrived so we had time to get orientated before our first operation. It was Kiel. At the time, I thought it was hell itself. In retrospect, it was a fairly easy do. The flak—remember, it was the first time I had been shot at—was a traumatic experience. No training had prepared me for such horror or nakedness. There was no cover. Not even a cloud. I was there, naked and exposed to what the Germans threw at me.

Eventually, most operations were almost milk runs. Hamm, Cuxhaven, Kiel, Hamburg.

The Ruhr was a bit different.

Then number thirteen—12A in my log book—Berlin. Fred and I agreed it was a bad omen. Bad enough to go to Berlin in a Wellington, without it being 12A.

There was a hushed silence in the briefing room when the target was announced. Even the most experienced crews were intimidated by the thought of such a deep penetration into the German Reich. And to bomb the German capital?

The briefing followed the well tried and practical formula. Our squadron flew off fifteen aircraft as part of a one hundred and twenty force. Only ninety-nine made the target.

PH 'R'—REAR-GUNNER SERGEANT D. ROBERTS was about number ninety-nine to bomb. The route in had been surprisingly easy. We had seen a lot of flak and searchlights on both sides of us. Presumably firing at aircraft that had wandered off course.

The target was different. We were late arriving and, as I said, number ninety-nine. Our predecessors had stirred up a hornet's nest in the ground defences. The flak was horrendous. Just about everything that could be fired at us was sent up. Intense light flak, its tracer sweeping the sky, hose-piping a murderous fire. Heavier flak bursting around us. And searchlights enough to make a picket fence. A tangle of spears that probed and searched like butchers' knives.

We stopped weaving for the minute it took to bomb. The bombaimer gave his order.

'Bomb Doors Open'.

It was wonderful to be flying straight and level—except that the ground guns could now predict us. The flak seemed to intensify. We were at twelve thousand feet, so the light flak could easily reach us.

I saw a stream of red tracer coming at me. It moved so slowly that I thought it had stopped in mid-air. It was directed straight at me. Fear gripped my bowel. This must be the end. The stream of tracer passed within a foot of my turret.

'Right. Right.' The bombaimer's voice loud and clear in the intercom. 'Steady. Steady'.

I screamed in my mind for him to say 'Bombs Gone!' It seemed an age coming.

'Bombs Gone!'

We were free of the bombs. Free of high explosive. All we had to do now was weave our way out of the target and go home.

For some reason, we did not weave. We continued to fly straight and level.

'Get weaving, you snotty-nosed bastard!' I screamed silently.

There was a sudden crash, a brilliant flash of light, and then darkness...

The distant voice of the wireless operator came over the intercom.

'I think he's bought it, Skipper.'

15

'Thank you, Wireless Operator.'

The snotty-nosed bastard is still there. At least he's weaving now. My thoughts were jumbled. I tried to think where I was. Then I remembered. But why was it so dark? And why did I hurt? I willed myself to relax and remember.

'Navigator to Skipper. Alter course two-seven-zero.' It was the navigator.

'Skipper'. Bullshit! Bloody Skipper! Who the hell does he think he is? My thoughts sounded crazy. Was I crazy? Flak happy? And why did I hurt so? My head and my guts. I could not believe there was so much pain. And the darkness. It was intense.

I passed my hand across my eyes; my gauntlets felt rough against my nose. There was a glimmer of light. I moved my hand again. The light improved. I put both hands to my head and wiped my eyes. I could see. Somehow my flying helmet had been knocked over my eyes, blinding me. But my head hurt and I vomited. The revolting mixture spewed into my oxygen mask, nearly choking me.

'Bombaimer to Skipper.' The voice in the intercom was almost deafening. 'Dutch coast ahead.'

'Skipper to Bombaimer. Roger.'

Bloody 'Skipper'. Bullshit! I was feeling a little better. Stronger. I began to hate again. And I could see, but the pain in my guts was no less. Blood on my face was dry and cracked as I

16

moved my facial muscles. My vomit was stiff with ice. And I was cold. Cold, hurting and frightened. Yes, and angry.

'Rear-Gunner to Pilot. What the bloody hell happened?'

I am sure the plane lost a thousand feet! The wings rocked and the nose dipped.

'Rear-Gunner? Are you alright?'

'Like bloody hell I am. And I'm not dead either!' There was a pause of several seconds.

'Skipper to Rear-Gunner. Good show.'

To give the snotty-nosed bastard credit, he had great powers of recovery. I smiled through the pain at my thoughts.

'Skipper to Rear-Gunner. Would you like to come out of the turret? I'm sure we can manage.' Quite a speech. He might even be human.

'No thanks. I'll be OK. What's a little pain to superman? It was said—and meant—sarcastically. There was no reply. My head hurt less. It was my guts that hurt.

We got a priority to land and the blood waggon was waiting at our dispersal. They bundled me up and hurried me off to sick quarters.

*   *   *

I lay with a great bandage on my head and a pain in my guts. Every time I breathed, it hurt. No bandages. Just an acute soreness.

17

I looked around and guessed it was about noon. 'Monty and Fred will be in to see me after lunch,' I thought. I must have slept after that, for I opened my eyes and there was Monty.

'Where's Fred? Still asleep?'

He did not answer immediately. He looked directly at me. His eyes, I remember, were very blue.

'Fred bought it last night.'

'What? Fred? Him? Not him! Not Fred! Dear Christ, please not Fred!'

I fell back on the pillows. My head felt it was going to explode. The muscles in my throat contracted and I choked against the sobs that welled up in me. Fred Cotton. Dead.

I looked at Monty and saw the tears overflowing from his tight closed eyes. Together we silently grieved for our friend and comrade.

Fred's Wellington, PH 'C'—CHARLEY was the only Twelve Squadron plane missing. The crew of 'S'—SUGAR had seen them coned by searchlights over the target and being strafed by light flak. They had watched helplessly as it spiralled to the ground and exploded. No parachutes were seen to leave the plane.

*   *   *

My wounds were not serious. The blindness had been caused by a glancing blow from a piece of shrapnel that had knocked my helmet over my eyes. Apart from breaking some flesh and creating a huge swelling and concussion, my head was fine. I had been unconscious from the time of bombing till the Dutch coast. A long time. The wireless operator had given me up for dead at the sight of all the blood running down my face.

My stomach had received a blow from a bigger piece of hardware. It had penetrated the turret-wall and struck the quick release buckle of my parachute. The buckle had taken the force but had pushed the whole apparatus into my stomach. I had a bruise the size of a soccer ball. Had it been three inches either way I would have been history.

*   *   *

I was out of sick bay in ten days and on light duties for another fourteen. During that time PH 'R'—ROBERT was reported missing from a raid on Cologne. The crew, Missing, Believed Killed. My navigator friend had gone. I missed him. And the pilots. I promised myself to be less critical of people from then on.

Monty and I were now in similar boats. Neither of us had a crew. We loafed around the squadron, trying to be useful. We walked or rode for miles over the rolling hills of the Lincolnshire Wolds. We explored the quaint little town of Louth a dozen times and each time seemed to find a pub nicer than the one before.

Crews were coming through to the squadron fairly regularly. Aircraft were lost with almost equal regularity, but individual crew members didn't always become casualties. The result was that, unless there was a gunner sick, neither of us operated for days, sometimes weeks, at a time.

By now, we were about the oldest members of the squadron. Nineteen forty-two came, with more visits to the Ruhr and the western industrial cities of Germany. Bomber Command was equipping more and more squadrons with the new four-engined bombers. Halifaxes and, more importantly, Lancasters. Twelve Squadron continued to dice in the old 'Wimpy'—a faithful, well-tried weapon, but carrying a six-man crew for a bomb load of only four thousand pounds. The Lancaster had a crew of seven with a bomb load of up to sixteen thousand pounds. We were impatient to get to a Lancaster squadron.

*   *   *

Our opportunity came with a new squadron just being formed. We joined the nucleus of ground and aircrews at a newly constructed airfield. Monty and I were together, he as mid-upper gunner and myself as rear-gunner. The rest of our crew were a mixed bunch of

20

Canadians and Australians.

We spent a month becoming familiar with each other and our new Lancasters. We flew every hour we could. Navigational and bombing exercises. Dinghy and parachute drills. Gunnery and signals. We became an efficient and well-knit unit.

Our first operation was a gardening sortie—code for mine-laying. We were to fly south to the west coast of France and plant five vegetables—mines—outside the estuary of the Garonne, leading to the city of Bordeaux. We were briefed to plant our vegetables from two hundred feet on a timed run at three-second intervals, course 360DG from the small headland of Point de Grave on the south side of the estuary. A straightforward operation. The German defences were expected to be light or negligible. Night-fighters were a possibility but we would be flying low, and over the sea for the whole time. It was going to be a long trip and would test all of us, especially in the navigation department.

The take off was faultless. We had a maximum load aboard but the four engines did not falter. The course was slightly west of south to Devon and our point of departure from the English coast, and then more westerly to avoid the German occupied port of Brest by twenty miles.

It was a lovely night. A full moon shone from an almost cloudless sky, its path stretching to infinity across the sea. Flying low over the ocean, the brilliance of the scene was breathtaking. Except that a marauding night-fighter could see us clearly against the silver sea.

I would peer along the fuselage and see the base of Monty's turret turning. Back and forth. First port and then starboard. Never too much; never too little. Never stopping the endless search for the enemy above. Monty, in his flowery prose, summed up the situation in a ditty as we left the briefing room.

'The Hun in the sun is no stranger;
But the Goon in the moon is our danger.'

We passed Brest without mishap. We could have been alone in the world. Not a living thing could I see. Not a ship. Not a single thing. The world could have been without life. The four Merlin engines droned on. The sea was an endless land of silver corrugations.

There was little chatter on the intercom. Our Australian sergeant pilot, 'Bonzo', was adamant.

'If you've got something to say, say it. And then button up. We don't want an Aunty Maud gossip session.'

The crew agreed. The result was minutes of complete silence. Silences when I would search and, as I searched, think. Thoughts of my past and plans for my future. Of the discussions with Monty and his utopian city. Of the violent trade we were engaged in. And dead friends. I thought of Fred. Monty and I seldom spoke of him, but he was in our thoughts often.

There were also times when I could only think of the fear that constricted my bowel and made survival the only thing in my consciousness. When I vomited with sheer funk. Cold, fatigue and loneliness, when I thought death would be a blessed relief.

'You might see the blast furnaces of Bordeaux at any minute, Swanny.' Our navigator, talking to the bombaimer.

'Roger, Tiny. Thanks.' Then silence.

'You're right, Tiny boy. They're on the port bow. Must be twenty or thirty miles.'

'Forty-five miles. Alter course to zero-niner-zero in three minutes, Bonzo.'

'Roger.'

Heading into the dropping zone.

'Alter course zero-niner-zero. Now.' The navigator's voice loud and clear. The Lancaster banked onto the new course.

'Coast ahead.' There was no waste of words.

In less than a minute I saw the shadow of land. Breakers rolling onto the beach as far as I could see.

'Alter course three-six-zero. Now.' The Lancaster banked again. We were over a long lake. A road to port. Dim lights of a vehicle.

'Look out for the point. It should come into view any second.' The navigator's voice was calm and confident.

The engines droned on and the dark shadows of earth took shape. Fences in the fields. An occasional farm-house. Sheds. Winding lanes.

'There it is. Dead ahead. Bomb Doors Open!'

I saw the railway lines before I saw the train. It was puffing north. The direction of the dropping zone. I was fascinated. It looked like a toy as we flashed over it. A small town to port. A few lights. One was blinking. A message? I read the letter. DOT DOT DOT DASH—'V'. The victory sign. Some bold Frenchman cheering us on.

'Steady. I'm counting. And one and two and three. And one and two and three.' I saw the splashes as the mines dropped into the water two hundred feet below.

'Vegetables planted. Bomb Doors Closed!'

I saw the flashes on my starboard beam, a stream of yellow tracer creeping towards us. A searchlight lit the sky and I aimed at the base of it. It took two long bursts before it went out. Tracer was still coming up. Some close. Another stream joined the first. I fired at the ship and felt the deep 'Crump!', 'Crump!' as the 40 mm shells found us somewhere towards the front of the plane. We were soon out of range and an alteration of course took us out to sea again. We were still very low.

'Navigator OK?' It was Bonzo, checking up

on the crew. He checked us one at a time.

'Monty?' No reply.

'Monty? You OK?' Still no reply. I turned my turret and looked at the base of Monty's. The moonlight filtered through his perspex. It was not moving. A foot hung limply. Lifeless.

'Blue. Get back there. He may have pulled out his intercom.'

'Roger.' The wireless operator was on his way aft. I dreaded what he would find. I knew Monty would not pull out his intercom. And that foot? I waited.

'Better get back here, Swanny, and give me a hand. Monty's been hit. He looks bad.'

There was no reply. Swanny would be on his way to the midupper turret. I cursed myself. It seemed an age before we heard anything.

'We've put him on the rest bed, Bonzo.' Swanny was panting. Monty was a big boy.

I fought down the urge to call out and ask how he was, but I had a job to do. I did my best to block my mind off from the fate of my friend. I searched the skies above and the sea below. We still had a long way to go.

'Monty's in a bad way, Bonzo. Shot up in the chest and head. We've given him a shot and stopped the bleeding. He's out cold. We've wrapped him in the spare chute as best we can.'

'Goodo, Swanny. Get back forward now. Keep an eye on him. Tiny, when we clear Brest give me a course for the nearest airfield in England. I don't give a stuff where it is. I want the nearest one. OK?'

'Roger, Bonzo.' There was nothing else any of us could do. We just had to get him to a hospital.

The moon was low in the west as we touched down at St Eval in South Cornwall. We had radioed ahead and an ambulance followed us to the dispersal. I didn't ask if I could go with him, just clambered into the back in full flying gear. I sat close. His eyes opened as I looked at him. He seemed to smile with them. His lips parted and he was trying to say something. I bent over and put my ear to his lips.

'Go and see my people.' The words were soft—a croak really—but they were unmistakeable. His hand was outside the blanket and I took hold of it.

'Yes, of course, Monty. Didn't we make a pact?'

Monty died a few hours later. I got my CO's permission to take him home. I sat with him as we travelled north to Inverness. The baggage waggon was cold and uncomfortable but the guard kind and sympathetic. He gave me a stool to sit on and I shared his sandwiches. It was a long journey. I watched over Monty as the baggage, mail and milk churns were stacked around his coffin. We changed trains at Inverness and had to wait for the train to Stromeferry. The two of us, in the station-master's office. I lived on insipid tea and sandwiches, but I refused to leave him. It was not that I was afraid of something happening to him. It was just that at that moment I was not ready.

We travelled on the slow train to 'The Ferry', as Strome is known in the highlands. The little push and pull engine puffed its way through romantic sounding names like Strathpeffer, Luichart, Achnasheen and Achnashellach. The scenery was magnificant. Monty was coming home to where he and his forebears had been born and lived for three hundred years.

We reached Stromeferry and were given priority. The estate sent a cart drawn by two Clydesdales to the station to meet us and take us to the family kirk above Kishorn, overlooking Lockalsh. A beautiful place. Wild and beautiful. Some of the older villagers and former retainers carried Monty into the kirk and he was laid out for the night. I stayed in the local hotel. Mrs MacNess was ill.

'I'd noo advise yee t' go yon. She canna abide strange folk. Her mind, yer ken. She no knoos what is gai'en on since the death o' the young laird wee Monty. Orch, it a muckel shame. The poor wee thing.'

The poor woman had collapsed when she'd heard the news. I subsequently discovered she never recovered, and died a year later, believing her son was 'away south of the border, but was soon coming home'.

Monty was buried in the family crypt next

day. The wee kirk overlooking the loch was crowded. The nearest RAF station sent a firing party and Monty was buried with full military honours. The family had lost another in battle.

I caught the first train south. I had said my good byes.

I still had a promise to keep. But more of that later.

CHAPTER THREE

DUSTY'S HATE

For the most part we didn't really hate the enemy. We didn't like him much either. We certainly didn't like being shot at. Of course, we pranged them as hard and as best we could, but hate? No. Not in my experience anyway. That was, not until we came back from leave in June 1943.

We had just completed our tenth operation. Essen it was, and we had lost two aircraft and crews. This had shot us unexpectedly to the top of the leave ladder. Six days operational leave was good under any circumstances. A quick shower and a change into our best blues, and we were on the bus to Lincoln. A farewell drink at The Snake Pit—Saracen's Head to the locals—and we were at the station, catching trains to our various destinations and the joys

28

of rest and recuperation. Hic!

'Dusty'—Sergeant David Miller to you—was our Wireless Operator. Even by our standards he was young. We all were. Ridiculously young. I was an ancient twenty-one, but Dusty, he was the baby of the crew.

His home was in Shoreditch in the East End of London. 'On the fird floor of Shaftsbury Billdings. A lot ov cowncill flats they are. Reel cowsy, if yer know wot I mean. Sniff!'

It was not that he had a cold or a runny nose. It was that each blast of dialogue invariably ended with a sniff. A nervous habit I suppose. He always spoke in a short burst of clipped words, heavily laced with the cockney idiom.

Dusty's father was a carpenter. Dusty never called him 'father'. It was always 'Me ole man' or, at best, 'Me Dad'. And his mother was 'Me ole dutch' or 'Me Mum'. She took in washing and ironing from the little pub around the corner. They both enjoyed a pint of 'arf and arf'—half mild beer and half bitter—at weekends. A glass of Guiness or, in his mother's case, a glass of port when funds allowed. The Saturday night sing-songs were their favourite outing and Mr Miller's repertoire of music hall ballads made him popular in the public bar most Saturday nights.

Well, it seems that Mum and Dad were in the public bar of The Dog and Whistle on the Saturday night of our leave. Dusty? 'I took me tart to the flicks in the 'igh Street, didn't I?' Sniff. So he was well clear of the tragedy that followed.

The siren sounded halfway through the main feature. It was Clark Gable and Jean Harlow in *China Seas*.

'Reel ixciting, it was.' He remembered it well. He and his girl had stayed holding hands in the back row until the ack-ack battery on the docks opened up. Only then did they disentangle themselves and run hand in hand to the Underground and the shelter it offered.

It wasn't what Londoners would call a heavy raid. 'Not like the blitz, it wasn't.' But one of the bombs landed fair and square on The Dog and Whistle. Just before closing time.

'It must 'ave been a big 'un, 'cos the 'ole Dog an' Whistle was just a bloody great 'ole in the bleedin' grownd,' sobbed Dusty as he told the story. He was offered compassionate leave but refused it. 'Wot's the bleedin' point? There ain't nuffin' to bloody bury. All the poor sods jus' bloody disappeared.'

So after seeing his older sister set up in the flat in Shaftsbury Buildings he returned to the squadron a day early. Of course, he was there when we all arrived.

We could see that something was amiss as soon as we saw him. He looked upset. Not his usual chirpy self. It took a while for the plucky little cockney to tell the whole story. What could we say? He was the baby of the crew, but

30

only by a year or so.

He was changing before our eyes. Gone was the cheeky grin and the ''Ow do, ole mate'. The light seemed to go out of his eyes. His shoulders drooped; his personal hygiene and appearance raised comments from the authorities; and worse, he began to take his drinking seriously. It stopped being fun. It was becoming a habit—or perhaps a need? His work however, was better than ever. He was at the wireless section genning up on all the latest procedures and information. He was the first of us to see the battle order and raved if our names were not on it. Sleep was his only respite and this was often disturbed by mutterings and groans.

Before that leave we would all laugh and jostle each other after the run up and checks prior to an op, or as we stood around the rear gun-turret, gossiping and urinating. Operational pees, we called them. Well, not really, but words to that effect.

Lately, Dusty was seen prowling around the dispersal picking up debris. Brick bats, bits of metal, odd lengths of ammo belts, lumps of wood, bottles, rocks. All sorts of junk. And carefully stowing it near the flare chute below the mid-upper gun-turret.

Now one of the tasks of a Lancaster wireless operator on an operational sortie is to station himself at the flare chute during the bombing run. This is so he can throw the manual release on the words 'Bombs Gone!' from the bombaimer. This ensures the release of the photo flash, should the automatic system fail. No one fancied flying around with one hundred pounds of volatile magnesium sitting with a primed barometric fuse in the middle of the aircraft. This pyrotechnic is timed to explode in the air at the moment of the bomb's impact with the ground. As it was synchronised with the aircraft's camera, it gave an accurate photograph of the bomb's strike.

Just before the run up to the target the wireless operator would disconnect his intercom and oxygen leads, plug into a portable oxygen bottle, and make his way aft to the flare chute. Once there he would reconnect his oxygen to the aircraft supply, plug in his intercom, and tell the crew he was in position.

The wireless operator's walk aft was potentially hazardous as he could stumble or get wounded while out of communication with his crew. The portable oxygen bottle had a life of only twenty minutes. Not long for the operation that was expected of him. A clued-up rear-gunner could check that he was OK by simply turning his turret abeam and peering into the fuselage. Generally there was enough reflected light from the flak bursts and search lights for him to discern a moving figure.

On these forays Dusty knew the drill. He never took chances. He would take up his position and listen for the bombaimer's 'Bombs Gone!' He would then throw the short lever and, as the flare shot down the chute, sing out 'Photo Flash Gone!' Then he would reverse his earlier drill and get back to his normal crew position. Lately though, this was delayed as Dusty hurled down his collection of junk.

I would catch glimpses of him with arms moving like pistons to get all the rubbish onto the target area. I sometimes imagined that I could hear him shouting obscenities down with it. Remembering, perhaps, the bomb on The Dog and Whistle.

The rest of us took this as Dusty's 'thing'. If we had thought about it seriously we would have said that perhaps it was a fairly healthy outlet for his hate. Frankly, we didn't take it seriously. In fact, we thought it rather a joke, to the extent that we often contributed pieces of bric-a-brac we found lying around.

It culminated on our last operation of the tour. Berlin of all places. Dusty was on his usual prowl and had quite a large collection for this special trip to the Big City. Then he found the railway sleeper. Well, it looked like a railway sleeper. Dusty staggered a bit under its weight as he carried it to the aircraft. He borrowed the crash axe from my turret and split and trimmed the thing to fit the flare chute. What a pantomime! Even Dusty laughed. A rare thing these days. Then up into the aircraft with it, and he stowed it with the other junk. An even bigger pile than usual.

The route to Berlin was a series of dog-legs, making feints at the Ruhr and Hamburg. Then south-east towards Leipzig. We came into the target from the south-west. This, we hoped, would confuse the night-fighter defences on the run in.

The German night-fighter command must have waited for a definite commitment by us. Once we were on that final run in they were amongst us in earnest. Two Lancasters were shot down in the time it takes to say this. One to port and one to starboard. We must have been exposed as the first one exploded in mid-air. I fought down the urge to give a combat manoeuvre that would take us out of this inferno. My right eye burned from the glare of searchlights and flares. I remembered to cover one eye in an attempt to retain some night vision for when we got clear of the brightness of the target area.

I found myself singing Gracie Field's song *'Sing as we go, and let the world go by'*. I sang as loud as I could. No one could hear me—my intercom switch was off. I don't know whether it helped. I had only got to the second verse when I heard the cry, 'Markers Dead Ahead!'

The pathfinder force were using *Parramatta* ground marking that night. The lurid reds and greens of the target indicators added to the already brilliant scene, silhouetting us against their glare. The flak was increasing and I knew it would soon be intense box barrage, as our window prevented the enemy's guns from ranging accurately. And so it was.

The German ground-gunners would set the fuses to burst at a prearranged height, point their guns at a fixed angle, and fire. There was no need for them to sight. The guns were arranged so that they filled a box of sky with exploding shells. Mostly it was the horrible flashless 88 mm shells. You couldn't see them until you had passed them. But you felt them. There was some heavier stuff, too. Blinding flashes of light which we knew exploded into decapitating steel fragments. The two together would toss us about with a constant blast.

I was singing again as I heard Dusty's voice over the intercom. 'I'm orf to the flare chute, Oats. OK?'

'Righto Dusty. Take it easy. We've still a bit to go.'

A searchlight beam passed over us. Will it come back? It did, but didn't find us. Thank God for window. While my turret was on the port beam I gave a quick glance down the fuselage. The scene was brilliant. The whole interior was lit up like a Christmas tree. Every one of the thousands of rivets was a pinpoint of light, illuminating the internals of the Lancaster. It was brighter than daylight. In the moment I watched I saw Dusty plugging in his intercom. As I swung away his voice confirmed that he was in position.

Just below and astern a Halifax disintegrated in a ball of orange-yellow flame that dripped like liquid fire and fell slowly to earth. There was no time to think of the crew. We were lit up for what seemed hours, exposing us to God only knew what. I saw a ME-110 night-fighter pass about five hundred yards across our stern. Too far away for a shot. The danger of collision with other bombing aircraft would have been a real risk had we corkscrewed in the confines of a bombing run. I didn't even mention it to the crew. I just watched and prayed and, yes, I was singing again. Crazy? Or was it 'whistling in the dark'? Except of course, it wasn't dark.

'We're coming up to the markers, Oats. Hold it as it is.' The bombaimer's voice was a reminder that I was not alone, as I often felt I was at the very tail of the plane. There were others sharing this time of cold, lonely torment. Hundreds of others. A rear-gunner in each of the six hundred and twenty bombers on the raid. The noise. The cold. The loneliness. And the fear.

'What a crazy way to earn a living.' How many times had I thought that. And yet—?

'Bomb Doors Open!' My turret was on the beam so I spared a glance for Dusty. The way he was crouched over the flare chute made him look like an ancient gnome sitting over a ghostly fire. I got the turret moving again. A

36

movement above showed a Lancaster just a hundred feet or so up, his bomb-doors open, the load clearly visible in the glare of the searchlight. The bombaimer was staring down at me! I felt I could see his smile beneath his oxygen mask. I was about to sing out a warning to Oats when his bomb-doors closed and he banked to port.

'Christ! Is he going round again? A real gutsy bastard, that.' This from Jerry, the mid-upper gunner. As the friendly plane banked away I saw its letters plainly: AR—'F'. An Australian from 460 RAAF Squadron.

'Thanks, Aussie.' I whispered my thanks. I had been bombed once by one of our planes. Not a nice way to die.

'Those bastards deserve a bloody gong.' It was Jerry again. He was as relieved as I was, but more vocal.

'Cut the cackle, blokes.' Probably Oats, our pilot.

'Left left.' The bombaimer's voice was loud and clear. We could hear his breathing. Like the rasp of a rusty saw on wood. 'Spot on. Steady. Keep her coming, cobber. Steady. Bombs Gone!'

Then almost immediately, unmistakenly, Dusty's 'Photo Flash Gone!' Not long now.

'Bomb Doors Closed.'

There was no let up of the flak. A Halifax was coned in half a dozen searchlight beams and was twisting and weaving in his efforts to

37

get clear. Oats was trying to compensate for the buffeting we were getting from the near misses coming our way. A German Fokker Wolfe-190 fighter dived through the flak. It flashed underneath us. A cat's eye fighter, sent to catch us silhouetted against the fires. They flew into us regardless of their own side's aggressive anti-aircraft fire.

'My God! They always hunt in pairs! Where's his mate!' Fear sweat oozed from my armpits as the thought struck me. I swung the turret. Willing myself to stay calm as the panic threatened to overwhelm me. 'Please God. Spare me this one last time.' It was a fervent prayer.

Another aircraft exploded above and astern. I couldn't make out what it was. Probably a Lancaster. Perhaps shot down by the other FW-190. I glanced quickly up to the fuselage. Dusty was still there but what the hell was he doing? No time to ask or look again. He was alive. That was all that mattered at this stage.

The German flak was still intense. The German gunners were throwing all they had at us. The target was still fully visible. A shell burst close and a lump of something starred the side perspex of my turret. The turret shook with the blow. That was a close shave. I had no time to examine the damage. My turret still worked so I kept up my search. Night-fighters were still around.

The searchlights were astern of us now and

lit up the sky. The red, white and green pathfinder indicators and the ground fires blazed a firework display that made boyhood memories of The Crystal Palace look like a backyard Guy Fawkes night. How could anyone still be alive down there?

Another shell burst just above me. I felt the blast and thought it was the end. A wisp of dark smoke was sucked into my open-ended turret. My eyes stung and tears flowed for a moment but soon cleared. How could anyone be alive up here? The way the Berlin gunners were firing at us I was quite convinced they wanted to kill us all.

'Any sign of Dusty?' Oats' voice was urgent. I looked up the length of the fuselage. He was still there. I could see him moving.

'I can see the little bastard,' I called. 'Christ knows what he is doing.'

My quick look revealed the little cockney with his oxygen mask tube stretched to snapping point. His intercom lead had pulled out of its socket and he was struggling at the flare chute. I had no time for a closer look. A searchlight passed over us. It travelled on and then crept back, feeling for us like the tentacle of some marine creature. It passed us again and went astern.

Soon the flak diminished and, as the target drew away, darkness enveloped us in its cold blackness.

'I'm back at me set, Oats.'

'Goodo Dusty. You OK?'

'Cawse I am. Wod yer fink?' Dusty's voice was his usual blast.

'What about the rest of you? Shout if you're not here.'

I smiled into my mask. The pilot was as pleased as the rest of us to be out of the target and on his way home. Like the rest of the crew, he knew we were a long way from being safe. We had all of Germany to fly over and Fritz would send as many of us to the ground in flames as he could.

As if to save me from being bored, a bomber was shot down a mile to port. The exchange of tracer showed the gunners had given a good account of themselves before their aircraft caught fire and plunged to earth. I did not see the fighter. Nor did I see any parachutes. They were too far away. There was another combat astern. A Halifax was lit up in the burst of the explosion that blasted it to a wreck in the air.

I had just reported this when I saw a shadow silhouetted against the distant glow of the fires. The twin engines could mean only one thing. A night-fighter.

'Corkscrew Starboard! Go!'

The words were hardly out of my mouth before we fell out of the sky in a diving turn to starboard. A stream of tracer shells pierced the sky where we had been. Jerry opened fire from the mid-upper turret. His tracer shot over my head in a stream. The Junkers-88 night-fighter

40

passed across my vision. I didn't consciously sight. I don't think I had time. The tracer from my four Brownings struck the tall tail fin. Not a killing shot. A lucky shot. Enough to drive him off. I hoped. Oats continued the combat manoeuvre and, at my command, resumed course.

We had possibly drawn blood but that was the best we could hope for. Another bomber disintegrated below us. The sky was lit up for a whole minute before it finally exploded on the ground. I tried hard not to watch it as it fell, but I was drawn to it like a moth to a candle. I cursed myself for an idiot. I cursed the Luftwaffe for not allowing us to bomb their capital unmolested. I cursed Bomber Command for sending me up to get cold, lonely and frightened. I just cursed.

Dusty's raving cut across my swearing. 'You should 'erve killed the bastard. Bugger dodging the sods. Kill the bastards.'

'Cut it out, Dusty.' Oats' voice was sharp over the wires.

The young cockney was silent for a moment. 'Sorry Oats.'

It was enough. There was nothing for us but to fly on. The Dutch coast was passed unseen below the clouds. Another bomber was shot down into the North Sea. There seemed to be no let-up. We were all tired. My eyes hurt from staring into the blackness, straining to find what I hoped was not there. The cold ate into my bones. The ice on the spittle valve of my oxygen mask needed breaking off frequently. Would this madness never end?

'English coast ahead'.

Joy. Oh joy. I could have kissed Pete. Eight hours of hell, cold and loneliness would soon be over.

Oats had been slowly easing the Lancaster down into the warmer air. We were below cloud and the darker coastline showed clearly as we crossed the unseen beaches and sand dunes of Norfolk. We could hear the airfield radio circuit and heard the safe return of friends.

Our turn to land came in due course and it was good to feel we were down—down for good. Number Thirty Operation safely completed. We had survived. I didn't mind that my back was jarred in the hard landing. I didn't mind that the bus was late arriving to take us to interrogation. We were all too happy to be on the ground, safe and together. All except Dusty.

'Wished you'd a got that bastard. Bloody Germans. 'Ope we kill the bloody lot of 'em. No bleedin' kiddin'. I really do.' Sniff.

'Hey, Dusty. What happened to you over the target?' Our pilot, Flight Sergeant Oats, passed Dusty a cigarette.

'Ooh me? Over the targit? Wot abart it then?' He looked a little guilty.

'Yes. What were you playing at in the flare

42

chute? You took so long throwing your junk down.'

'That? I couldn't get the bloody fing darn the chute, could I?' Sniff. 'Too bloody long it was. Well, almost.'

'What? Your railway sleeper?'

'Yes. Had to struggle wiv it a bit, didn't I?'

'How did you manage it in the end?'

'He nearly stuck it up me arse, that's how he managed it!' Jerry complained.

'That's right. I had to stuff it up into the mid-upper turret. The only way I could do it, wan' it?' Sniff.

'She'll be right. But don't let's tell the bloody Wingco.' Oats had us laughing as the crew bus arrived. I looked at the old Lancaster that had served us so well. Twenty of my thirty ops had been in that tiny gun turret. I looked at the recent flak holes and appreciated my good luck and the loyalty and comradeship of my crew.

'Come on, Pom.'

Almost reluctantly I got into the bus. The last thing I heard as I stepped into the dim interior was the metallic tinkling as the engines cooled in the cold dawn air.

We had a riotous party in the local pub that night and carried it over to the sergeants' mess afterwards. It was to be the last time we drank together. We were all posted to different stations next day.

Dusty volunteered to go straight to a pathfinder force squadron. 'Can't let the bastards get away wiv it, can I? Got ter keep on, 'aven't I?' Sniff.

He was killed in a raid to Konigsberg six months later. A nightfighter shot his Lancaster down. Only the rear-gunner survived. Dusty is buried with the others of his crew in a tiny East Prussian country churchyard.

'Rest in peace, Dusty. Your hate has spent itself. You have more than avenged The Dog and Whistle.'

* * *

When the war was over I was demobilised and, when in London in 1949, went to see Shaftsbury Buildings. 'Cownsill Flats. Fird floor.' I knocked on the door. It was opened by a young woman with a small boy hanging onto her skirt. It was Dusty's sister. I learned that she had lost her husband on the beach at Normandy on D-Day. She had invited me into the tiny flat. 'Reel cowsy, if yer know wot I mean.' I almost heard the sniff.

There, on the new radiogram, was a picture of the family. Dusty standing proudly in uniform with his mother, father and sister. Close to it was one of the seven of us around the old Lancaster. The little boy climbed onto his mother's knee.

'Ain't he like his uncle Davey, then? Ain't he though?' The proud mother stroked the little boy's hair. Yes he was. Very like him.

I left soon afterwards. As I turned at the end of the narrow balcony I saw the cheeky Dusty grin of old on the little boy's face.

'So long Dusty, old chum.' I was looking at the child but talking to his dead uncle. My old wireless operator.

I could hardly see for the tears in my eyes as I went down the grimy, gloomy concrete stairs to the dreary London street. I caught the bus for Victoria Station at the stop by a hole in the ground that had been The Dog and Whistle.

CHAPTER FOUR

ANGUS' WOUND

Hut 24, Number Two Site, Royal Air Force Station, Wickenby was a hive of conviviality. The five occupants were good friends, well used to the buffoonry and quick repartee that blessed this tin shed set in the midst of what was otherwise a dreary rural backwater of Lincolnshire.

There were five in a hut designed for three. All Flying Officers by rank, and all members of the same Lancaster crew. Because of this they had chosen to break the rules and move into the one hut. The Twelve Squadron adjutant had seen fit to turn a blind eye.

Their nationalities were as diverse as their

personalities. The pilot and bombaimer were Australian. The wireless operator was Canadian and the mid-upper gunner Rhodesian. This left the navigator. He was a Scot, so dour that he could have walked out of a Walter Scott saga.

Flying Officer Angus Ross, of the Clan Ross, was a quiet, laconic character. He despised the sassenach custom of drinking cold, lifeless beer, smoking the 'obnoxious weed', and the unchristian and unladylike habit of women's exposing things that should be for the sole sight of a legal husband. Bums, legs and bosoms to us more sub-human aircrew types. He was of a strong and sincere Presbyterian faith; born and bred on a highland farm on the rocky shores of Loch Shin in far north Sutherlandshire.

Although he had this strong aversion to English ale, he was not amiss to supping a dram of the real highland sustenance whenever time and availability made this possible. His preference was Heigh, but any genuine Scotch whisky would suffice in the days of wartime austerity. Not that he imbibed to excess. But on standdown nights he would tipple a dram wi' the best, and drink perhaps more than was prudent for such a pillar of the kirk.

On these occasions he would lapse into philosophical discussion about the merits of Home Rule for Scotland, the need to fight The Extravagances of Popery, or The Kirk o'

Scotland. All in the gentlest of spirit, with no rancour. As the evening progressed he would burst into some dirge of a highland lament, with unintelligible Gaelic lyrics, telling of his remote, sad, but glorious ancestry from the dawn of history. Nobody minded because nobody listened. As the evening wore on he would sit, quietly humming the monotonous dirge, a half-filled glass of whisky in his hand. 'Just to keep the fog of this den of iniquity from rotting me bones, yer ken.' That would be until someone began a game of mess rugby. Angus would then rise like a storm and be leader of every scrum. All, especially his crew, thought he was a credit to the squadron. Well liked and respected, especially as a navigator.

The pilot, red-headed Flying Officer 'Bluey' Desmond Moody, and his crew had joined Twelve Squadron on a bleak January day in 1943. The battle of the Ruhr was just warming up. 'Which one?' you ask. There seemed to be one on for the whole war. The crew—'Bluey Moody's mob', they were called—soon earned a reputation as press-on types.

Bluey flew his first op with the squadron commander. It was the customary familiarisation flight to give an aircraft captain his first taste of action under the wing of an experienced crew. It was Essen. The wing commander's aircraft got shot up by flak and lost its flight engineer, wounded. On the way home a night-fighter attacked them and killed the mid-upper gunner before the rear-gunner was able to destroy it.

The Wingco's aircraft was, in the words of Carl, the Canadian wireless operator, 'like a god-damned colander'. It was probably the best thing that could have happened to them at that time. Bluey took the whole of his crew out to view the wreck the next morning.

PH—'L' was sitting in a dispersal while engineers were trying to assess whether it was fit to repair. Riggers and armourers were swilling out the blood and oil from the shattered fuselage. The wintry sun shone through the shrapnel holes in the skin.

'Look at it, you bastards. This is what can happen to us. Or bloody worse. I intend to get home and sail my old man's boat on the Swan again. So keep your fingers out and let's pull together and beat this shit of a war.'

Whether it was the sight of the blood and the ruined plane or their pilot's unusually long speech that made them silent and thoughtful they could not tell. Whatever it was, they all admitted that the sight of 'L'—LOVE standing there, crippled, had a profound effect on them all. None of them needed Bluey's remark to tell them they must pull together. There were a well united and skilled crew, and they knew it. All they needed was operational experience. Each secretly prayed he would live long enough to get it.

Their baptism came two nights later. What a

baptism it was! The target was Essen again. The English daily tabloids claimed that the Germans had a hundred thousand guns defending the Ruhr. Essen was plumb in the middle of them. They weaved and jinked through the labyrinth of shell bursts, and somehow got home with only a few holes in their Lancaster and seven chastened crew members to show for the trip.

January passed into February. Then March. Twelve operations in their log books. 'Twelve A' was coming. Fate had been kind; their luck had held. No serious damage had been sustained to their aircraft and not a drop of crew blood had been spilt.

It was a chilly day. The days of rain and fog had given way to late frosts. The nights were now cold but clear. A high pressure ridge was dominating the whole of Europe. Flying Officer D. Moody and crew were on the battle order. They had done the checks on their aircraft—PH 'N'—NAUGHTY as it was called by the crew.

'Always wanted me own regular naughty.' Merv had to explain to the non-Australians that a naughty was an Australianism for an illicit sexual adventure. So *Naughty* the Lancaster was called.

Angus disapproved. 'It's noo the name I would ha' chosen. I'm thinking Neil would ha' been fine. There was a fine poet from the highlands in 1805. He—' A howl from six

49

throats drowned Angus' story. He shrugged his shoulders and was resigned to *Naughty*, even mentioning it by name in his letters home.

All the checks were complete. The seven of them were aghast at the volume of fuel being loaded into the wing tanks and the absence of the usual four thousand pound 'cookies' in the bomb-bay. They had never needed so much before and the big bomb was always carried. Where were they going that night?

'I don't care where we go. Just so long as we make it 'ome.' Reg, the English West Country sergeant rear-gunner, spoke for them all.

Briefing was at 1800 hours. Time for a spell of horizontal drill after lunch. The five retired to Hut 24 and settled down to sleep the winter afternoon away. The two NCO's withdrew to their hut close by.

*   *   *

The map on the wall of the briefing room drew them like a magnet. The zigzag of red tape across Europe showed their courses to and from the target. The large-headed yellow pin showed the target. Pilsen!

'What's at bloody Pilsen?'

'We're bombing the bloody brewery, mate!' Merv's answer to Sid, their flight engineer, had them all laughing.

The Wingco mounted the rostrum. He flexed his long pointer as a schoolmaster would flex his cane before a class of errant boys.

'Well chaps. Another maximum effort for Twelve. Tonight we are to destroy the Skodda Panzer factory in Czechoslovakia.' There was a rustle of movement throughout the room. 'As you can see, it is a long way and we will fly low-level in and out. Maximum height one thousand feet in the hope of getting below the enemy's radar and ground defences. We should be too low for effective night-fighter attacks. The route has been plotted to avoid high ground and defensive zones, so good navigation is essential. You will...'

The briefing went through the usual pattern. Apart from the distance and the low-level flying, it was similar to others they had sat through.

The crews filed out into the clear winter's evening.

'Better take a few extra sheets of bum paper tonight, I reckon.'

'A few? I'm taking a whole bloody roll.' It didn't matter who said it. It was enough to raise a laugh as they changed into their flying clothes.

'A dicey bloody do tonight, Angus. So keep on the ball, you bloody Jock.'

'Ach, Merv. It'll be noo so bad. If I get the chop youse can map read yer way hame, we'll be that low. Sure. You'll be able to read the road signs!'

They joked and jostled each other good-humouredly as they waited in the bright starlight. Each added his share to the puddle beneath the rear turret. It was going to be a long trip.

They piled in. Angus pulled the ladder up and checked the gyro compass. There had been no mention of trip twelve-A. No one was going to risk breaking their good luck.

It took several minutes to settle into their flying positions and check, yet again, their equipment. Everything was functioning properly. Intercom. Oxygen. Electrics. They only needed to start the engines and get airborne.

The four Merlins sounded sweet as they taxied down the perimeter track to the caravan at the mouth of the runway in use. The green light flashed at them. Reg turned his turret to beam and Bluey opened *Naughty* for all she was worth. The Lancaster shook as the engines gathered power. The tail lifted a trifle, brakes were released, and they were rolling. Faster they went. Soon the tail was in the air and the huge black shadow of PH 'N'—NAUGHTY was airborne and retracting its undercarriage.

'Flaps up.' There was no comment from the flight engineer. They knew the drill on the flight deck. The tone of the engines settled down to cruising speed. The throb of them almost soporific in the blue-black of the starlight.

Angus gave the course to fly with a minimum of words. They were on their way. The moon rose as they crossed the North Sea. The reflection on the water had Jerry, the Rhodesian mid-upper gunner, looking in wonder at the beauty of the scene. The sea was a river of silver corrugations, stretching back along the path of the moon. The black shadow of the Dutch coast was crossed at one thousand feet. Surf breaking on the shore. The pale white beam of a searchlight probed the sky and streams of red tracer shells crept slowly into the air to the north. A crew off course had flown over a defensive position.

The moon was reflected in the canals as they flew over Holland. Periodically, another Lancaster was sighted in the pale moonlight. Otherwise the earth was black. Not a light showed. No encouraging signal from the friendly Dutchmen. Nothing until the glint of a railway line in the moonlight. A good fix and a check on their navigation. Merv identified the landmarks and Angus' 'Fine! Fine!' showed they were on course.

Their track would take them south of the Ruhr then south of Frankfurt. Merv and Angus had the intercom to themselves as the landmarks were checked off. *Naughty* flew deeper into Hitler's Reich. Flying at a thousand feet was low and dangerous. The night was bright but there was little room for error. The navigation had to be almost perfect to avoid the high ground. And it was.

The full moon was straight ahead.

Landmarks stood out now. Roads, rivers, even houses in the brilliant light. Woodlands showed dark. Lakes glistened. It was fairy-like. As Angus had predicted, they could almost read the road signs.

'Keep an eye upstairs, Reg. More likely a fighter will come from above than below tonight.'

'Wilco.'

Angus gave the heading that would take them to the target. 'Fifteen minutes on this course, and we're there, Boy Blue.' The Sutherland accent was thick over the intercom.

Minutes passed. Night was still on their side. It was all so peaceful—so far.

'Markers ahead.'

'Can see.' Merv's voice cut through the silence. Bluey's reply was brief, as always when approaching a target.

'Course two-eight-five after the target, Blue.'

'Roger.' No waste of words.

The gunners scanned the sky above. There were several Lancasters visible as the bomber stream began to converge.

A stream of red tracer crept towards them. Slowly. Reaching them, it rushed by the wing, fast. More came up as they drew closer. Searchlights swept the skies, groping for the low-flying Lancasters. One caught 'N' but her groundspeed was too fast for it to more than briefly touch. Heavy and light tracer was criss-crossing above, behind and in front of them.

Tracer streams were passing close. There was a 'Crump!' as a shell found a spot on the plane. Sid was shocked to see a line of bullet holes appear in the fuselage in front of him. Before he could react, the perspex blister close to his head shattered, struck by a heavy machine gun bullet.

'Bomb Doors Open.'

'Bomb Doors Open.' Bluey repeated Merv's instruction.

'Right.' The pilot kicked the rudder bar.

'Steady mate. Steady. Steady. Bombs Gone!'

The plane rose, tossed like a coin in a giant's hand. The flak still came up. The blaze of multi-colours from the ground-markers and the red, yellow and white tracer was a firework display they would all remember.

The delayed-action bombs began to explode as they pulled away from the target. The pyrotechnic scene was incredible.

'You gotta see this, Angus. Get out here.' Bluey's voice was jubilant. The scene was a sight to invigorate a dummy.

Angus put out his reading light and pulled the thick curtain aside. He half stood, leaning up to look through the flight engineer's window. Then he collapsed at Sid's feet, striking his head on the metal step. He lay unconscious.

'Bloody 'ell.' The flight engineer looked at the line of small holes stretching up the fuselage to the roof of the Lancaster. There were flames coming from the navigator's bullet-shattered 'gee box'.

'Angus 'as been bloody 'it.' His Londoner accent marked, as it always was in times of crisis. Fear clutched his breast as he saw the flames. Like all aircrew, he had a dread of fire in the aircraft. He ignored his fallen comrade and grabbed the fire extinguisher, dousing the flames with a cloud of chemical powder. He dropped the now useless cannister and stooped over the fallen Scot. There was no obvious sign of a wound. Sid examined him closely and saw blood seeping onto the flight-deck floor.

'Getcher first aid satchel 'ere, Carl. Angus 'as bin shot in the bloody arse.' The Londoner had Angus' parachute harness off and was undoing his trousers when the wireless operator came forward with the satchel.

The shock of the bullet had released the anal sphincter and Angus' bowel content was well mixed with the blood that flowed in a stream from the wound. It was neither the time nor the place for a close examination. It looked horrible they both agreed, but not fatal.

Angus stirred and moaned. Carl took a capsule of morphine and plunged the needle into his friend's thigh. Between them they slapped a number of shell dressings over the wound, excrement and all, and got the navigator onto the rest bed.

'Angus OK?' Bluey's voice showed his concern.

'I reckon so. He'll have to eat his food standing for a while, though.' Carl pulled his leather gauntlets over the filth on his hands resignedly.

The flak and the target were well behind now. Merv was map reading and giving courses to the pilot. The Lancaster droned on, heading almost due west. The full moon was directly overhead and lit up the whole countryside. The gunners knew they were too exposed.

'Away wi' ye, Carl. I can navigate on me two feet fine.' Angus' voice cut through the intercom as he weakly thrust the wireless operator back into his seat. And navigate he did, and well. They were able to avoid high ground and defended zones. Soon they were over the North Sea. The gunners scanned the sky above and to the east. They knew they made a bold silhouette against the moonlit sea.

Angus had allowed himself to be laid on the rest bed again. He was weak from loss of blood and his exertions at the chart table. Carl had given him another shot of morphine and the Scot lay dozing beneath an opened parachute.

Wickenby Flying Control answered them the first time and gave them a turn to land. There were no priorities. There were too many wounded for that, and several dead. The German light flak and machine gunners had given a good account of themselves. The medical teams at the base were working at full pressure.

PH 'N'—NAUGHTY taxied round to its regular dispersal point. There was an ambulance backing to the rear door before the engines had stopped. Reg was sitting on the sill and saw the WAAF medical officer step from the cab. He put the ladder down and took her bag.

'He's up front, luv.' Reg's West Country experience was not up to coping with the unusual sight of a lady doctor seeing to a male casualty.

Senior Section Officer Christine Marsh thanked the rear-gunner and hurried forward.

Carl met her at the flare chute and helped her to the side of the wounded navigator. 'You lucky son of a bitch. You've got Christine to powder your bum.'

There was a cry from the rest bed. 'I'll no' have a lassie look at mar arrse.' He struggled in vain against the strong hands of Sid and Carl as they held him down. 'It's noo decent. I'll noo forgive ye. Ach please.'

It was too late. Christine had given him a needle of something and he lapsed into a murmur and then silence. He was quickly put on a stretcher and carried out to the ambulance.

The six remaining members of *Naughty's* crew watched the blood waggon disappear. They were standing away from their plane, smoking a much needed cigarette as they waited for the crew bus. All agreed it had been a long and hard trip.

'Well, that's got number firteen op art the bloody way, an' it.' They all laughed at Sid's comment. They had forgotten the dreaded twelve-A.

The six crew of *Naughty* were at sick bay early after lunch the next day. They entered the ward, stopped at the door, and laughed. Their navigator was lying on his stomach with his wounded seat sticking up into the air.

'Like a bloody poofta on a Saturday night when the fleet's in.' Merv's ribald remark had them all laughing again. Even Angus was able to raise a smile.

'It's fine for youse to laugh. I noo mind that. But I'll no forgive youse for lettin' a lassie look at ma arrse.'

The six of them were still laughing when SSO Marsh shushed them out of the ward.

Angus was soon out of sick bay. It was only a flesh wound. The small caliber machine-gun bullet had passed through both buttocks without touching a vital spot. There were four wounds where the bullet had passed through the cleavage of the Scot's delicate seat.

'The only bastard I know with five holes in his arse.' Carl was forgiven for his remark.

What Angus found harder to forgive was his friends' ribbing him to make an honest woman of Christine. They could see that the MO and their navigator were getting a little more than friendly.

The crew of *Naughty* finished their tour with a long but relatively uneventful trip to Turin. Their flight over the Alps in the moonlight would always stand bold in their memories.

There was quite a party at The Adam and Eve in Wragby next night. Drinks were flowing fast, and before Angus could start one of his dirges, Sid piped up with the scene over Pilsen.

'He nearly knocked me arse over kettle, 'e did. I looks darn at 'im and finks "Cor, Angus 'as 'ad it," like. I turns 'im over and takes 'is strides darn, dun I? Cor. Yer should er seen 'im. Blood and shit everywhere.' He took a long swig at the pint pot in his hand and faced the crew again. 'I gets this toob I sees in the satchel and looks at the long bloody nozzle at the end. I looks at Angus' arse and finks, "There's only one place fer that". So I stuffs it up 'is arse for 'im, dun I? And I squeezes 'ard. Wot a bleedin' mess. Just like a bleedin' rainbow, 'is arse was. Blood, shit and gentian bloody violet.'

Merv and Bluey almost choked on their beer. Even Angus gave a rue smile. They all agreed the party was a success. The Scot, slightly the worse for a dram, sang a wild lament for them all the way back to the mess.

They went on leave. Bluey, Carl, Jerry and Merv went to Loch Shin and spent two weeks fishing for trout. And drinking. 'The nectar o' the highlands. Noo like that horrse pee you

60

drink in the colonies.' The four colonials were not surprised when Christine Marsh arrived to meet Angus' parents.

Angus and Bluey each received a Distinguished Flying Cross. The dour Scots navigator went as navigation leader to a newly formed squadron and collected a bar to his DFC for the completion of a second tour. Bluey and Merv flew a second tour with 460 Squadron, RAAF. Carl and Jerry were shipped home to train new birds in their homelands. All contact was lost with Sid and Reg. We learned years later that both had been lost on their next tour. Shot down on a raid to Berlin.

*   *   *

1987. The five met in Perth, Western Australia for the defence of the America's Cup. They sailed into Fremantle Harbour on Bluey's yacht *Naughty* after a day's sailing, watching the competing yachts. They were reminiscing about 1943, recalling the danger and friends who hadn't made it.

'Well. We made it. We beat that shit of a war. Now help me get this bloody mast down.'

'Always the bloody skipper, ain't he.' Merv's dig at Bluey had them laughing again. It had been a fun day. One laugh after the other. Like the days in Hut 24.

The yacht passed under the Fremantle

bridges and motored up river to the yacht club. Five ladies watched their husbands walk across the lawn. Christine was the first to greet her husband. She and Angus had retired from the farm on Loch Shin. Two sons managed the flocks of black-faced Scottish sheep. They lived quietly in a cottage and were established pillars of the wee Kirk in the Glen.

With arms linked the ten walked into the bar.

'Just one to wash the salt away.'

Their laughter caused several heads to turn. The smiles that followed were understanding. Bluey had been a member since he was a boy. And anyway, wasn't he the commodore?

CHAPTER FIVE

TAKE ONE. YOU NEVER KNOW

The BBC announcer's voice was flat and emotionless.

Five hundred aircraft from RAF Bomber Command bombed Essen again last night. Extensive damage was inflicted on industrial areas and railway marshalling yards. Numerous fires were seen to be burning. Forty-two planes failed to return.

The sergeant's mess at Royal Air Force

Station, Wickenby, Lincolnshire was crowded with young aircrew. They listened in silence. Two of their squadron's aircraft were among the forty-two missing. Fourteen of their number were absent. With luck they were able to parachute to safety, or worse, ditch into the unfriendly, though neutral, North Sea. Some were undoubtedly killed and others taken prisoner.

A few of those fortunate enough to bale out would be picked up by the Dutch, Belgian or French underground and eventually find their way home via Spain or Switzerland. But these would be very few.

Flight Sergeant David O'Riley took a long pull at the pint glass in his huge fist. One of the missing men was Flight Sergeant William Jones, DFM, a particular friend of his. They had first met at the recruiting office in Regent Street on a foggy London day in November 1939. Both had survived a hectic tour on Wellingtons, followed by a rest period as instructors in the same training unit. They had arrived together at Wickenby to join 12 Squadron.

Yes. They were great friends. They had also met two girls together and the four had married the same day. Because 'Jonesey' was Baptist, the ceremonies were performed in different churches, but each had been best man to the other. The two couples had honeymooned together in Ross-on-Wye.

And what a laugh that had been. Dave smiled as he remembered.

Jonesey—he had collected his gong on his first tour, after shooting down two night-fighters the same night—was a person of considerable initiative. The flight sergeant sipping the pint was convinced that, if he had been able to bale out, he would survive. They had talked over the possibility many times.

'Jonesey would make it.' The thought comforted the big man as he drained his glass.

Dave, as he was called by all who knew him, came from Irish stock though his accent was pure cockney. His father had been on holiday in London when war was declared in 1914 and, being Irish, young and able-bodied, volunteered for the London Irish Rifles. On his only leave from France he had met and married David's mother and after the war they had settled in London.

David was born in 1919 and grew up a child of the streets. He was not much of a scholar and happy to leave school at fourteen. Being a large and rather ungainly youth, he had no trouble finding employment as a bricklayer's apprentice with a prominent firm of London builders.

'Sure, he's as clumsy as a colt, and as gawky. He may as well work like a horse. It'll do him no harm. He might even learn a thing or two while he's at it.'

David had enjoyed his working years. He

was popular with his workmates, had a good sense of humour, could hold his beer, and was good to have on your side in a fight.

The news of him joining the air force had come as a great surprise to his parents who, when they thought about it, had felt their giant of a son was sure to join the Irish Guards. But David had other ideas.

'No f—n' mud in the f—n' trenches for me,' he would say, as he recalled the stories his father had told of Flanders in 1914.

'Not f—n' likely. I'll 'ave my war in the comfort of an aeroplane and keep me bleedin' feet dry.' And so far he had.

The two Mrs' Jones and O'Riley still lived with their parents in London and only saw their husbands on leave. Being aircrew, these leaves were more frequent than those of most servicemen. Every six to eight weeks found them home.

'Escape and Evasion' were important topics at the lectures they attended on days when flying was impossible. There were talks of escape routes, explanations of the escape gear they carried on all operations, maps, money, emergency rations, and the like.

On one occasion they were given a talk by an NCO who had evaded capture by being befriended by a prostitute. He spent two weeks with her until the underground spirited him into Spain and so back to Britain. He was now spending a few weeks touring the bomber squadrons to speak of his 'ordeal'. Passing on hints for dealing with the problems of evasion and recovery from a dose of gonorrhoea contracted in enemy territory.

Dave and Jonesey wondered about the possibility of a similar experience. They were both newly married and the thought of an extra-marital adventure was not attractive. Neither was the thought of capture and the years in a prisoner-of-war camp.

It took several enjoyable pints of mild and bitter, and no little talking, to convince themselves that perhaps sleeping with the lady—any lady—was better than the other possibility.

But the thought of bringing home venereal disease! That would never do.

It was Jonesey who first came up with the idea of carrying condoms. 'A bloke can't be too careful, can 'e?' And Dave had to agree.

So the pair invested in a pack of the popular brand. They had a good laugh discussing where to secrete them without soiling them and at the same time not making their presence too obvious. The shell-dressings they carried in a purpose-built pocket of their battledress was the very place.

It didn't take them long to unpick the stitching and put the rubbers snugly beneath the khaki cloth. Then restitch and replace in the pocket.

'Better not puncture the frenchy, Dave, or

some bloody Dutchman might come chasin' after yer wiv a bleedin' pram and your little bastard.' Jonesey's joke had them both laughing.

And so it was. When they were in battledress they always had the condoms with them. When they went on leave they emptied their pockets, including the field-dressing, and took their battledresses home to be dry-cleaned.

*   *   *

It was a week or two later. David and his crew had just landed from another raid on the Ruhr. Three of their aircraft had failed to return. Another bad night for Twelve Squadron. Squadron Leader 'Pop' Huggins approached them as they were leaving after interrogation.

'You chaps have been able to jump to leave ladder because of tonight's losses. So you are on leave from 0800 hours this morning.'

Well, one man's sorrow is another man's joy. The crew of 'G'—GEORGE hurried to their huts for a quick wash, a meal, the early bus for Lincoln and the trains to their various homes.

Dave hurried through his shower. He changed into his best blues. His soiled battledress and an assortment of dirty clothes he bundled into a battered suitcase. With this in hand, he went to the sergeants' mess for a quick breakfast.

He had to run for the bus and fell into it, to

the laughter of his crew. They split up at the railway station. Only Digger, his Australian bombaimer, was going to London with him.

The two were able to find a seat in a smoker and spent the journey smoking, talking, and eventually sleeping. A neighbour had to waken them when they got to King's Cross, so soundly did they sleep.

A quick drink at the station buffet woke them up enough to catch their respective tube trains. Dave was heading for Paddington; Digger for the flesh pots of the West End.

It was about two-thirty when David arrived at his wife's parents' little terrace house off Praed Street. His mother-in-law answered the door to his knock. She was wiping flour from her hands as she opened it.

'Davey, boy.' She threw her arms around his neck to hug him. As he bent, she placed a moist kiss on his unshaven cheek. 'Gawd bless yer. Come on in.' She tried to brush the flour from his tunic, but laughed as she only spread more onto the blue cloth. ''Ere, look. Ain't I makin' a bleedin' mess of yer nice uniform,' she laughed again. 'Come on in, then. I've got the kettle on. Or would you like a bottle of brown ale? Dad's got one under the stairs.'

The big rear-gunner stooped as he walked down the narrow passage to the kitchen at the rear of the house.

''Ere. Sit yer down.' She pulled a well-stuffed chair towards the fire as she spoke.

She was a small, bird-like creature, but her frame encased a heart as big as the house. She must have been pretty when she was young, thought Dave. Her figure was still trim, though there was little flesh on her bones.

She and her husband had lived in this little house all their married lives. Had reared their six children within its walls—no mean feat for a couple who had to exist on the wage of a council worker.

'It ain't much, I know. But it's regular. Know what I mean?' she would explain to whoever inquired.

There was a silence as the tea was poured and passed to the weary young flyer. Sara swung around from her pastry-making as the cup and saucer fell. David woke up with a start.

'Sorry, Ma. I must've dropped off.' He tried to mop up the spilt tea with a none-too-clean handkerchief.

''Ere. You get up them apples and pears. I'll see to this 'ere.' She nearly pulled him to his feet. 'Orf wiv yer nar. Your Betty won't be 'ome from 'er war work till six. So you've time for a little kip before she shows 'erself. Come on.' She bundled him, unprotesting, through the tiny door that led up the narrow stairway to the three bedrooms above. 'Lie darn in our room. I've got to clear our Mabel's things art of Betty's room before you and yours can sleep decent tonight.'

He entered the marital bedroom and settled

69

himself into the lumpy, feathered warmth, his clothes an untidy heap at the end of the old couple's bed.

It must have been seven o'clock when he woke. He could see it was dark outside as the blackout curtain had not been drawn. A light shone from downstairs, a slit glimmering beneath the closed door.

In an instant he recognized the howl of despair, mingled with anger, from his young wife. He leapt out of bed and was down the stairs, clothed only in issue underwear. It didn't help when he struck his head on the lintel.

'There y'are. Yer great lump of lyin' humanity.' Betty O'Riley's eyes blazed with anger through her tears. 'You rotten lyin' sod. 'Ow could yer, and we ain't been married a year yet?'

He just stood there in a state of shock as she dived for him. Her finger-nails drew blood before his large hands could hold her. She fought like a demon, kicking and screaming enough to wake the whole neighbourhood. He held her to him as she exhausted herself, her cries a mere sad-sounding whimper.

''Ow could yer, Davey? 'Ow could yer do this to me?' Her tear-filled eyes looked up at him.

'Do wot, for Christ's sake? I've only been 'ome a couple of hours. Wot 'ave I done?' He was all surprise and doubt.

'Wot's this 'ere, then?' Betty's voice rose an octave and threatened to erupt into anger again. She made a grab at his battledress trousers. 'I got 'old of these bleedin' things to take to the cleaners like you like me to do. I thinks, "I'll empty the pockets, like".' Her voice broke at this point. 'And I found these.' She held up the field-dressing with the telltale condoms secreted in its folds.

'Is that all?' He made the mistake of relaxing his grip on her.

'Is that all? Yer great faithless bleeder. Is that all? Ain't it enough ter know me 'usband's a lecher? Doin' any tart wot drops 'er drawers?' Her strength renewed, she was about to attack him again.

'Is that wot yer reckon? Yar silly little moo.' His words were soft and caressing. 'It ain't like that at all.' His arms were about her and he was trying to find her mouth as she tried equally hard to avoid his lips.

Eventually they met and he swept her onto his lap as he sat in one of the overstuffed chairs.

'Let me tell you about it, then.' And he did.

She was weeping quietly as he finished his tale.

'Now wot the bleedin' 'ell are yer 'owling about?' His voice was gentle. 'Wot is it now, Betty love?'

'Yer wouldn't, would yer?' she sobbed.

'Wouldn't wot, sweetheart?' He was puzzled.

71

'You wouldn't …' She hesitated. 'You know. To one o' them tarts?'

'Of course I wouldn't,' he lied. 'They make us take them fings. In case, like. I wouldn't. I'd rather be captured, if yer know wot I mean.'

She was smiling through her tears as the old couple peered around the door.

'You two finished, then? 'Ad a real barney, then, 'ave yer? Nice makin' up, though, ain't it?' Ma winked knowingly at Davey.

*   *   *

It was late at night. They had made love and slept a little and made love again. He had dozed off when her lips woke him.

'Davey?'

'Wot?' His voice was sleepy.

'I won't mind. Not if it means yer won't be taken prisoner. Know wot I mean, luv?' Her head was on his chest and her fingers fondled the soft, fair hairs. 'Perhaps you'd better take one, just in case, like.'

It was as well she did not see the grin on his face as he closed his eyes again and slept.

*   *   *

Jonesey turned up a couple of months later.

'Well, wot happened then, Jonesey?'

The air-gunner winked at his friend. 'Wot don't tell, don't lie, old mate. But I'll tell yer

72

this for nothing, Davey boy. I'll always take one. Yer never knows.'

CHAPTER SIX

LEAVE IT TO ME, ROBBIE, SIR!

I first noticed Nobby—Sergeant Herbert Clark, RAFVR, Air-Gunner—as he was sitting in a class of gunners at the operational training unit, Hixon, near Stafford.

He sat at the back of the class and tried to be as inconspicuous as possible. I was lecturing on the marvels of the modern multiple-gun turret and explaining the drive of the hydraulic motor. Once or twice I noticed that, even when using very basic terms, I was not getting over to some of them, particularly Nobby.

I defined centrifugal force using the simple analogy of the mud leaving the wheel of a car and sticking to the mudguard. The smile on Nobby's face told me the shaft had got home, to him anyway.

I should say that I was an instructor at this time, serving out a period of rest after completing a tour. In the few weeks the pupil crews were with us I was able to get to know them. Some more than others. Nobby I got to know better than most.

73

One didn't enquire too much into their personal lives, but Nobby was much older than most of the lads—and they were lads for the most part. Average age, about twenty. Nobby was thirty-five, and even sported a few grey hairs at the temples.

Inevitably, the dreadful day came when I had to examine them on their ability to operate and do minor maintenance on the turrets. Nobby was not doing too well. His written paper left a lot to be desired and I decided to give him an oral examination to see if he could pick up his marks. I asked several questions on the technicalities of a particular turret, and one on a hydraulic motor.

'Tell me, Sergeant. What do you know about centrifugal force?' I spoke plainly and waited for Nobby's reply.

He looked me squarely in the eye and said, after some hesitation, 'Aw, Mr Robbie, sir. That's when the shit leaves the wheel and sticks to the mudguard, ain't it?' I had to agree.

Nobby scraped through his theory but excelled in his practical tests. His air-firing and flying drills were well above average and his ability to manipulate the turret controls were excellent. His dexterity at stripping and assembling the Browning machine-guns was amazing.

He left the unit in due course, and joined Twelve Squadron at Wickenby.

*   *   *

Nobby and his crew of Canadians had completed twelve operations when I joined the squadron. I arrived and reported to the gunnery section. Almost the first face I saw was Nobby's.

He greeted me with, 'Hello, Mr Robbie, sir. 'Ow are yer, then? 'Aven't seen yer for ages.'

It was good to see him again. I was about to start another tour and his friendly greeting did much to help me over the apprehension of a further spell of operational flying.

I had no crew at this stage, so hung about the gunnery section, catching up on the latest combat reports and intelligence information. I noticed that Nobby was a constant presence, seeming happy to be around rather than avoiding the office. It was not long before we struck up a friendship of sorts. As it happened in those days, our conversations would turn to family and pre-war occupations. I asked Nobby what he had done to support his wife and four children.

'I was a carter on the LNER. You know, the Lunnon Norf Eastern. The railway.'

I remember he was puffing away at an old pipe at the time.

'Yes. Me and me old 'orse would set off from St Pancras in the mornin' and travel around, dropping orf parcels all over Lunnon. Knows the smoke like the back of me 'and, I does. Me old 'orse did too, bless 'im. He got killed in the blitz, poor old bleeder. Lovely old bloke 'e was, too. Reel faithful, 'e was. Know wot I mean, then?'

In this vein, I got to know Nobby Clark. I felt I knew his wife and each of their four children. I learned all about their little council house in Bermondsey, the trouble they had with their neighbours, and the progress the children made at school.

When he had not been flying the night before, Nobby was invariably the first into the section office. In the cold winter, it was Nobby who lit the stove, scrounged the coke to keep the place warm, swept the floor and cleaned the windows. If any chores, some of them none too pleasant, had to be done, it was always, 'Leave it to me, Mr Robbie, sir.' And I'm afraid I did.

*   *   *

It was a bleak February day when we were briefed for a daylight raid on Duisburg. I was with a crew by then and was sitting behind Nobby at the briefing. I shared a hut with his Canadian pilot, navigator and bombaimer. Along with my own pilot, also Canadian, we were a happy if sometimes noisy crowd when the mood was on us.

The briefing proceeded normally until the end. It was then we learned that one crew was to carry as an observer a notable BBC war correspondent. We saw this gentleman sitting in the VIP seats to the front. He looked huge and prosperous in his neat gabardine battledress, and he fairly exuded wealth and comfort, used as we were to frugal wartime conditions.

The raid was relatively easy. Lots of flak, of course, but our fighters kept the Luftwaffe at bay. All the aircraft made the target, and all returned safely to base.

In the officers' mess that evening I was able to speak with our guest and, rudely, I suppose, asked him the going rate for a correspondent to fly on a bombing operation. He was very friendly and didn't mind my question a bit.

'Oh, only a hundred pounds, old boy, but we hope it will increase soon.'

I was amazed. Nobby was getting the princely sum of eight shillings a day. For a four-hour operation this worked out at a shilling and three pence a trip. The price of two pints of beer.

On one of our many conversations I asked Nobby why he never went out with us on stand-down nights to enjoy a beer or two and the high jinks that invariably followed.

'Aw, Mr Robbie, sir. I can't afford it, can I? Not wiv a missus and four nippers ter feed. Eight bleedin' bob don't go far, does it? One round of drinks and Nobby's more broke than me muvver's bleedin' heart.'

It didn't upset the phlegmatic cockney. It

was just a fact of life that he accepted as readily as he did his flying duties.

Nobby and his crew had done twenty operations in their tour when they went on leave. I remember the time well.

The old gunner came up to me and asked if I wanted him 'to bring anyfing from the ol' smoke.' I asked if he could bring an ounce or two of my favourite tobacco from a shop in Regent Street.

'Corse I will, Mr Robbie, sir. I knows the bloke wot owns it, dun I?' And he probably did. He hurried to the bus like a schoolboy on an outing.

His crew returned on time but there was no sign of Nobby. Two days went by and he was posted Absent Without Leave. An offence only marginally less severe than desertion. He arrived on the third day.

As luck would have it, I saw him alight from the bus and hurried across to him.

'What happened, Nobby? Were you sick?' I hoped he was, as I could think of no other reason to get him off the charge.

'Nar. Nuffin' like that, Mr Robbie, sir. Nuffin' like that at all. It was my Lil, wasn't it? Yer know. Me missus.' He was finding it difficult to find the words.

'Was she ill, then?' I asked.

'Well, not exactly, Mr Robbie, sir. Not really ill, that is.' He changed the battered fibre suitcase in his hand to a new grip.

'What the hell do you mean "Not really ill"?' I was getting annoyed with his excuses. It was so unlike him.

'Well, the fing is, Mr Robbie, sir. When I gits 'ome, see, she 'as 'em on, if yer know wot I mean.' He looked really uncomfortable.

'Has what on?' I insisted.

'The rags, Mr Robbie. Yer know. The mumflies.' He blurted it out almost angrily.

I could have died with the shame of my intrusion, but I suppose the ice had been broken.

'She wasn't fit until it was time for me to get back up 'ere.' He looked at the suitcase in his hand. 'She asked me to stay fer a coupler days. I couldn't refuse 'er, could I? Anyway, I didn't want to. I knew I could get the bloody chop on this next op, and well, I just stayed with 'er.'

I told him to report to the guardroom and square things there at the earliest. I wondered if something could be done for the old gunner.

I thought it over during the night and approached the Wingco privately. I'm sure the he was secretly laughing his guts out at my stammering attempts, but I couldn't tell from the expression of official countenance. He just kept tapping his pen on the desk-top and looking very severe. Very severe indeed.

So severe that I began to think I should not have meddled.

The Wingco stopped his tapping and looked at me.

'Well, Robbie. This is a new one for all of us. The silly bugger has got to be clobbered, of course. But damn it. It could happen to any one of us. And has for all I know.' He laughed at his afterthought. 'I'll see him later this morning. Meanwhile, I'll give it some thought.' It was a dismissal for me. I saluted and beat a hasty retreat.

Nobby was on the carpet later that morning. I stood at the back of the room. I suppose I could have been called the Prisoner's Friend. Anyway, I was there to give support, if only meager, to my carter-cum-gunner comrade.

Nobby was marched in hatless. Number, rank and name were given, and the charge of Absent Without Leave was read out. The squadron commander had on his severest look and eyed old Nobby up and down.

'Well, Sergeant Clark. What have you to say to the charge?' His voice had the sound of dread in it.

Nobby stood stiffly to attention. Eyes straight to the front. It was as if he had not heard. The OC looked into his face.

'Well. Sergeant? What have you to say for yourself?'

I could see the boss was getting impatient, and I mentally willed Nobby to say something.

'Nuffin' sir!' The sound was like a rifle shot.

'Come, man! You don't go AWL for nothing. You must have some excuse!'

I sensed the old man was giving Nobby a

chance to fabricate a story.

'Well, sir. When I gits 'ome, my Lil—that's my wife, sir—'. And it all came out. Just as he had told me. Every minute, personal detail, and a lot more.

I spotted a fly on the ceiling and kept my eyes fixed on it. I dared not look at Nobby and spoil his monologue. The Wingco's pen was going tap, tap on the desk-top.

There was a silence for a moment when Nobby had finished the last intimate syllable. The squadron OC stopped his tapping and coughed.

'Well, that is a very likely tale, Sergeant. But this is an operational squadron and we cannot afford to have aircrew, any aircrew, just being absent with leave, for any reason. Do you understand?'

'Yes, Sir.' Nobby's eyes were to the front. His back, ramrod straight.

'Very well, Sergeant. Severe reprimand! Dismiss!'

Nobby's 'Fank you, sir,' was lost in the marching out procedure. The door closed behind the former prisoner and escort. I heard the Wingco chuckle as the adjutant came in.

'Oh, Smithy. I have just bawled out our friend Sergeant Clark. Here, take this charge sheet and burn it. He deserves to get away with it. But he must never know or the whole bloody squadron will try it on. We must keep this very much under our hats. OK, Robbie?'

'OK indeed, sir. And thank you.' I saluted and left the office, my feet floating on air.

*   *   *

About two weeks later we were briefed for a night raid on a small city in the Black Forest region of Germany. Frieburg. It had never been bombed before and the ground defences were expected to be light. Night-fighters were their usual, unpredictable menace, and were considered the real risk.

Nobby's Lancaster took off just ahead of us. I waggled my guns in salute as he passed and I saw him return my farewell.

It was a last farewell. PH 'E'—EASY was missing that night. Sergeant Herbert Clark, RAFVR, Air-Gunner, and his whole crew was gone. Believed Killed in Action.

*   *   *

My wife and I toured Europe this last summer and I looked in on the city of Frieburg. There is no sign of the bomb damage. All the beautiful old buildings have been restored.

My thoughts were very much with Nobby. Later, in the Reichswold Forest war cemetery, I found his grave. He is buried in a joint grave with all his old crew.

A sad day for me. My final farewell to a natural, very humble, honest gentleman. I can still hear his, 'Leave it to me, Mr Robbie, sir.'

CHAPTER SEVEN

JEESE. WHAT AN OP THAT WAS!

For three days we were confronted by that empty bed. The bare dressing-table and the chest of drawers cleared of family photographs. The wall above stripped of the scantily-dressed pin-up. A clean ashtray. Empty of the revolting cigar butts he used to stub out so aggressively. Though the air in our hut was sweeter with his absence, we missed that wonderful, maddening, hard-swearing, rumbustious son of a bachelor.

We had shared the dreary Nissen hut with him during the equally dreary winter of 1944–45. Close support bombing raids for the allied armies invading Europe were frequent at that time. The weather had to be near perfect for each operation, so there was much standing by until the sky cleared. Briefings were often followed by cancellation at the last minute.

All this meant being confined to quarters, for sometimes days at a time. The enforced conditions encouraged a spirit of comradeship. A tolerance, albeit reluctant at times, of the fads and weaknesses of one's hut-mates.

Canadian Flying Officer W. J. 'Spud' Murphy's bed had been vacant since his non-return from a raid on Leipzig just three nights before. A sad reminder every time we entered Hut 21.

*   *   *

'Brew', or 'Big Bill Brewster' as he was called—a Flying Officer pilot in the Royal Canadian Air Force—and I, his reargunner, had flown as part of a daylight bomber raid supporting the British and Canadian armies advancing towards the German homeland. It had been a bad trip. Our navigator had been wounded by the vicious flak over the bomb line—that infamous line separating the opposing armies in France. It was the usual filthy flashless 88 mm stuff. Being flashless didn't make much difference in daylight. The oily-looking black puffs desecrated the clean blue sky.

It was bad that it happened so early in the trip. We were only slightly damaged and well able to fly on. Poor old Norm, our Canadian navigator, was in some pain even with the shot of morphine that Mac pumped into him. Anyway, it was safer to press on with the rest of the eight hundred or so bomber force. To turn back would have meant leaving the gaggle—the loose formations we flew in those daylights. Then, of course, we would have been without the support of the unseen fighter screen that was there to protect us. So press on we did, with poor old Norm full of morphine and Mel the bombaimer—another Canadian—checking the navigation. Not that there was any problem. We only had to follow the gaggle to the target, and then all the way home. A piece of cake, navigation-wise.

We met lots more flak over the target and got rocked rather than knocked about. I don't think we were hit. But, with all the holes in us when we got home, who was to know when or where we collected them.

It was time for tea when we got back on the ground. By the time we got old Norm safely into the blood waggon, been interrogated, rushed around to the sick bay to check that our navigator was in good hands, and had a wash (surprising how dirty one got up there), we were late for the operational meal.

It had been a pre-dawn take-off, and it didn't cheer us up too much when we heard we were on the battle order for another daylight next morning.

We were a tired pair as we ambled down to Hut 21. Night was closing and it was cold. Betty, our little WAAF batwoman, had drawn the blackout curtains and, bless her, lit the fire. We felt the warmth of it as we entered. Brew turned the light on but I think I beat him to my bed. I fell backwards onto it and lay spread-eagled, just enjoying the stress and fatigue oozing from my body.

It must have taken some minutes to notice that Spud's old bed had been made up. There were new photographs on the dressing table. A very pretty girl and, as if to balance it, the picture of an elderly lady, lace cap and all. Apart from these, there was no sign of the new occupant.

After a while, we stirred ourselves and went for a shower and then a nap before going back to the mess for dinner. No one could enlighten us as to the new fellow in Hut 21.

We were tempted to have a small beer before turning in but discipline prevailed and we settled for a lemonade instead. There was still no sign of our new hutmate.

Brew had arranged for us to be called at 0400—time to get up, rustle the NCO members of our crew, and have a leisurely breakfast before the mob invaded the mess. I hardly read a chapter of my whodunnit. When I muttered 'Goodnight' to old Brew across the room, all I got in reply was a deep throated snore. I switched the bedside light off and was asleep in no time. It had been a very long day.

I woke the instant I felt the hand on my shoulder. I opened my eyes. The reek of re-cycled alcohol hit my face. The light was on and I beheld a pale, sharp-featured face surrounded by a mop of unruly long, lank, dark hair. A forage cap was over one ear.

'I say. Do forgive me for waking you. But

you see, I'm drunk and it's my twenty-first birthday. Many happy returns.' He burped into my face.

I think I was about to explode when he ambled over to Brew's bed. I could still hear his snores. Our drunken intruder got as far as, 'I say. Forgive me . . .' when there was a grunt like an angry bear.

'F—off, you drunken son of a bitch.' Brew was sitting bolt upright. 'Christ! It's only one-thirty. Get to hell out of here!' The old skipper was really getting his longjohns in a knot.

The drunk was not put out in the slightest by this poor response to his well-intentioned introduction. 'I say. Don't be cross old man. It's my birthday. Don't you know?' He burped again, as if to emphasise it.

'I don't care if it's the bloody Pope's birthday. Get to bed, you bum.'

We were both wide awake now.

'Let me introduce myself.' Our drunken intruder drew himself to his full weight, staggered backwards, almost colliding with the stove, and collapsed onto what we presumed must be, now, his bed.

As he didn't move, I got out of bed and took the prostrate officer's shoes off, removed his necktie, and let him sleep it off. The light was out again and I was between the warm sheets in a flash. I had just snuggled down when I heard Brew's snore. 'A couple of hours to go,' was my thought as I drifted off.

It seemed only moments before we were woken again. It took the sight of the fully-clothed Flying Officer lying on Spud's old bed to remind us of our disturbed night.

'Let the drunken son of a bitch sleep it off. He'll feel bad enough when he wakes without us making it worse for him.' I detected some ambivalence in Brew's tone as we went out into the cold darkness.

The early morning chill and the frosty air augured well for the coming operation. The sky was brilliant with the stars and we had no trouble finding the hut of our still-comatose crew. It was with no little difficulty that these gallant souls were lifted from the arms of Morpheus and goaded into some semblance of life. Eventually, they were on their feet and the pair of us hurried to the showers in an attempt to regain our original time advantage.

We weren't the first for breakfast, but early enough to avoid the crush. We even had time for a leisurely smoke and a yarn with old chums before it was time for briefing.

The map on the dais wall revealed that we were revisiting yesterday's target. This was always bad news, as it generally meant we had not pranged it too well the time before. Also of course, friend Jerry was apt to be rather angry with us.

The briefing followed the well-tried formula. Nothing unusual was expected. No new techniques were to be introduced. The fighter cover was to be the usual high-level stuff and there were to be strafing aircraft to shoot up the flak-batteries ahead of us.

The only unusual thing was the Op itself. It was a piece of cake. Everything went according to plan. In spite of the strafing aircraft, the flak was its customary aggressive norm. Enemy fighters were fended off by our escorts. The PFF marking was spot on. Altogether, the prang was a success. At least for us. Fifteen of our aircraft were missing. Perhaps we had just been lucky.

We landed in time for tea, hurried through the interrogation and winding-down routines, and got to the mess in time for a good meal.

Exhausted, we pushed open the door of Hut 21. Music was erupting from an old wind-up gramophone. A figure was seated in the chair, feet on the table, arms beating the air in time with the music. We stood at the door, dumbfounded.

The record ended with a crescendo and culminated in a roll of drums and a clash of cymbals. The Flying Officer lifted the needle off the record and leaned back in his chair with a deep sigh.

We must have made some movement at this stage for he leapt to his feet with a startled cry.

'I say. Hello. Are we room-mates?' Then he looked shamefaced. 'I say. Did I make a complete ass of myself last night? I am sorry.' The emphasis was on the 'am'.

'No,' was my immediate response. 'Not last night. But this morning we could have gladly killed you.'

'This morning? Oh! I see what you mean! Stupid of me. Sorry.' The tall Flying Officer shuffled his feet with embarrassment.

'Don't ever do that again or, by Christ, you'll have a squeaky voice for the rest of your life.' Brew's voice had a chastening effect on the young pilot.

'I say. I really am sorry. I honestly can't remember too much after leaving the Gordon Arms. I suppose my crew brought me home. Here, that is. I really am sorry. But one is only twenty-one once in one's life, isn't one?'

'Thank Christ one is. Only once,' muttered Brew sarcastically.

He stepped toward us as we moved further inside. 'I'm Barrington-Jones. Charles Barrington-Jones. But everyone eventually calls me Bunny.' His rather pointed features and prominent, protruding front teeth certainly did give him a rodent-like look.

He was looking directly at us. Long, lank hair fell over his eyes in spite of the Brilliantine. The multi-coloured neckerchief beneath his chin gave him a Bohemian appearance. He extended his hand. He had long, sensitive fingers and his handshake was warm and firm.

'Hello Bunny. Welcome to the 21-Club. This is Brewster, my driver. He is house-trained, believe it or not, and answers to Brew. I am his super-human rear-gunner. I answer to Robbie.' I moved swiftly away to avoid Brew's foot aimed at my rear.

'Take no notice of the little bastard. He's full of bullshit.' Brew was shaking Bunny's hand. 'Little men always have high opinions of themselves,' he added, good-humouredly.

We didn't talk much that first night. The preceding Op had been relatively easy for us, but it had been tiring, so after a quick shower we had our heads down. Bunny, out of consideration for us, or perhaps because of his indiscretions the previous night, made himself scarce. We both slept until Betty woke us with a cup of tea.

A night operation was planned for that night. We weren't on the battle order, so we could relax: a trip to Lincoln for some shopping, see a film perhaps, and visit some of the city's pubs.

The Op was scrubbed just after lunch, so the bus was crowded. Most of the aircrew were anxious to get away for a few hours to let off some steam. Perhaps take a girl out or simply get away and feel safe for a while. We all did different things for different reasons. Or were they so different? Who knows?

Bunny and his crew were to fly on a bombing and navigational exercise, so he was still in Hut 21 as we left. He seemed none the worse for his night of revelry, and was getting out his old gramophone as we left.

91

We did our film in town. It was Humphrey Bogart in *Casablanca*. The show finished in time for us to have a quick meal and several beers before it was time to catch the bus.

The bar was still open in the mess when we returned, so we went in for a nightcap and a yarn with whoever was at the bar. An hour passed very pleasantly. We talked of many things—mainly flying and the war. We wound up before midnight and headed for our beds and a well-earned rest.

* * *

We were briefed for another daylight two days later. An early take off again. Bunny was to go as second Dicky—second pilot with an experienced crew. He questioned us about our feelings when we flew, confessing that he was terrified at the prospect of an Op. He seemed relieved when we also confessed to being afraid.

'Jeese. I always wear three pairs of underpants and the stain still comes through.' Brew's ribald comment did much to put the subject in a humourous vein and Bunny was laughing with the pair of us as we entered the briefing room.

It was to be a fairly deep penetration attack. Fighter cover was going to be difficult and would involve overlapping waves of combined RAF and US Army fighter planes. The flak was expected to be intense, so altogether it promised to be an eventful trip.

'Reckon I'll need another pair of longjohns today.' Brew spoke for us all.

The Lancaster that Bunny was flying in was directly behind us for take off. I saw him plainly as we taxied towards the runway and returned his cheerful wave. The take off was problem-free and we circled to gain height over the airfield. Bunny's Lancaster was sighted several times, the letters PH—'Q' plainly visible in the early morning sunshine.

The six hundred strong Lancaster force altered course at Cromer, the point of departure from the English coast. I caught sight of 'Q' QUEEN—*Queeny* to the crews— away out on our port beam, slightly below us.

When we crossed the Dutch coast we were all at about twenty-one thousand feet. The drill was to pack ourselves fairly tightly in the gaggle. Each aircraft flew independently. There was no regular formation. Just 'pack in tight and lob out the window'—strips of tin foil we threw out to spook the enemy radar.

I had no trouble picking up Bunny's kite. It was always to port and now level with us. Like us, it was flying the regulation straight and level to minimize the risk of collision. The skipper of Bunny's aircraft, Squadron Leader 'Poppa' Huggins, was a real old pro. He had an ambition to be the oldest pilot in bomber command.

'It doesn't worry me that I'm not the best. I'll be content to be the oldest.' His witticism was the joke of the squadron. This was his fifty-third Op.

The odd puff of flak was shot at us as we flew over the German lines in France. Not much, but enough to tell us that friend Jerry was not going to make things too easy for us. One salvo of half a dozen shells burst between *Queeny* and ourselves. Another Lancaster, UM—'D', passed right through them, apparently unscathed. I thought of Brew's remark to Bunny at briefing and would put money on it that there was some stained underwear in that aircraft.

We were well into Germany now. The flak was getting heavier. Smoke was coming from a Lancaster on my port up. I could see its letters. AR—'H'. An Australian aircraft from Binbrook. The damaged plane held on a steady course. The smoke increased momentarily, then stopped. It had already feathered one engine and I was surprised it was able to maintain height and speed the way it was. I gave full marks to her pilot and engineer.

Flak was all around us. Grotesquely-ugly black elongated puffs that looked so benign but harboured a dose of death for any aircraft unlucky enough to be hit by one.

'Q'—QUEENY was now close on our port beam. Slightly astern and only about fifty yards away. I guessed it was Bunny standing behind the engineer because he was waving. I returned his salute by waggling my guns at him.

My God, the flak was fierce now. The Australian Lancaster was hit again and loosing height rapidly. It flew below us in a shallow diving turn to starboard with flames pouring from it. It watched her go and, with relief, saw six parachutes blossom from its stern. I looked in vain for the seventh. The kite exploded before number seven, probably the pilot, bailed out.

Our new navigator had no sooner logged this than Mel's call of 'Bomb Doors Open!' heralded the target proper. His breathing was loud over the intercom. Rapid, excited breaths. I caught a glimpse of Bunny's kite still on our port. Level and slightly astern. Their bomb doors were open too.

The flak was around us like a cloud. The 'Crump!' and the 'Bump!' of it all buffeted and jinked us around. Brew had his work cut out holding us straight and level for Mel's bombing run.

I was fascinated by the antics of PH—'Q'. Bunny's plane was bobbing up and down and rocking its wings with near misses that came their way. It was not a comfortable thought to realize that exactly the same was happening to us. The flak was as heavy as I had ever experienced. Our Canadian bombaimer's voice had a waver to it as he gave directions to

Brew.

'Steady as we go, Brew. Steady.' A flak shell burst so close it tilted a wing and must have disturbed his aim. 'Bombs Gone!' Mel's voice came over the intercom, quickly followed by, 'Bomb Doors Closed!'

It was a relief to feel that we had no high explosive aboard now. At least we would not explode as the unfortunate Aussie had. Or would we?

I glanced quickly down the fuselage to check that Mac, our Australian wireless operator was OK at the flare chute. Then a quick look for 'Q'—QUEENY. There it was. Its bomb doors closed and, like us, heading out of the target.

Sid, our new navigator, had just given an alteration of course when Bunny's Lancaster caught a flak shell just in front of the nose. It passed through the smoke in a second and seemed to pull in its neck, so to speak. When I next looked, the front gun-turret was askew and the nose blister missing. And part of the cockpit canopy.

The crippled Lancaster weaved erratically and lost a bit of height. Then the nose pointed skywards, beginning a steep climb. Seconds later it was on an even keel, flying straight and level. Whatever was going on in the machine, things were in hand and everything was under control, however uncomfortable.

The flak did not ease up for some time. Another Lancaster was shot down on our starboard quarter. Two parachutes bloomed in her wake. Then it went into a spin and disappeared from my view.

Bunny's *Queeny*, meanwhile, was managing to hold height and course, but its speed was dropping off.

'We'll fly escort to her as soon as the flak lifts.' Brew's voice was breathless from his exertions at holding the aircraft steady in the flak bursts.

Eventually—it seemed like hours—the flak eased. Just a desultory, almost lazy flak puff. Then we were through it. I looked back at *Queeny*. She was maintaining height but dropping further astern. A few crisp commands from Brew and Jack, our soft-spoken Yorkshire flight engineer, adjusted our engine revolutions. It took some minutes for PH—'Q' to catch up.

Brew waggled our wings at him. To cheer him up, I suppose. We eventually formatted on him, flying slightly high and on his starboard side.

As we closed we could see the extent of the damage. The whole nose section was a mess. The mid-upper gun-turret was unmanned, although it looked serviceable. The rear-gunner was OK, and he waved energetically to confirm this. We couldn't make out what was happening in the cockpit. The pilot was hunched over the controls and seemed to ignore us. He did not respond to our waving.

There was nobody else on the flight deck. It was as if the Lancaster was manned by the uncommunicative pilot and the energetically friendly rear-gunner.

We were flying just above stalling speed. Brew had to juggle the controls to keep in station, yet not fall out of the sky. Other Lancasters were passing continuously, generally above us.

At long last the Dutch coast came up. Then the North Sea, cold and grey below. Brew waived the golden rule of RT silence and tried to call. *Queeny* on the radio. If the damaged Lancaster received us, he was not telling. The pilot just sat huddled over the controls.

The English coast came into view. We were now directly over *Queeny*. There was still no response. As we passed over the Norfolk Wash, Brew called Wickenby Tower and put them in the picture. We picked up the airfield circuit and orbited as per regulation.

Not so PH 'Q'—QUEENY. She was straight through the funnel and onto the runway in an almost perfect landing. We all saw her veer off the runway and eventually stop. We watched as men and vehicles converged on her, and wondered what they would find.

At last it was our turn to land. Brew did not make his gentlest landing that day. But not to complain. We were home. And as I said later, 'Any landing you can walk away from is a good one.'

It was not until we were in the briefing room that we were able to discover what had happened to *Queeny*.

The shell that had carried away half the nose had killed the bombaimer and wounded the other three on the flight deck. Pilot, flight engineer and, of course, old Bunny. Our hutmate had got off lightly however, receiving only small shrapnel wounds to the arms and shoulders and perspex splinters in his face. His eyes had escaped serious injury.

'Had my eyes closed the whole time!' he said. 'Right from the time I saw the first flak shell burst. I thought perhaps they would go away if I pretended they weren't there.' His toothy grin belied the fear he must have felt and the truth of the situation.

'Poppa' Huggins received serious wounds to his head and chest. And the engineer was wounded along the whole right side of his body.

'Poor buggers. Wouldn't surprise me if they were both grounded after this.' It was days after Bunny had returned from sick bay that his story came out. We were grounded by the weather and were sitting around the hut stove. Bunny was very low. The experience had shaken him more than he, or the doctors, realized. He was sitting on the edge of his bed, holding one of Brew's Lucky Strike cigarettes between nervous fingers. He looked at us.

'There was a gigantic crash and the cockpit

was filled with black, oily smoke. I was thrown through into the navigator's position and landed in a heap on his chart table. I must have bounced back immediately. I felt the body of the flight engineer against my legs. He was in a bad way, poor chap. I left him in the care of the navigator and looked at the skipper. He was bleeding profusely from the head wound and looked really bad. They both did.'

Bunny fumbled for another cigarette. I gave him one of mine and lit it for him. His fingers shook and his lower lip trembled as he continued.

'I had a bit of a job releasing old Poppa from his seat harness and getting him from behind the controls. The old fellow just would not let go. My intercom plug had come out and I didn't think to plug it in again for a moment. I remember my oxygen tube was so stretched I thought it was going to snap.' He smiled weakly at his little joke, and wiped his eyes with the back of his hand. 'Anyway, I got the poor blighter out and handed him over to the wireless operator, who magically appeared at this point. The kite was behaving like a demented bronco.'

'I know. I thought you were going to prang. You looked as if you were going to stall the bloody thing.' I was sitting on the edge of my chair as I recalled the sight of it all.

'That must have been when I was struggling to get him out of his seat. He hung onto those controls like grim death. I was able to get behind the controls and level the kite out. Meanwhile, the mid-upper had come forward to help and he reported that the bombaimer had had it. Poor bugger was a mess. The whole of his head and back were blown away. He must have died instantly.'

He finished his cigarette and was looking for another. I lit one for him and passed it over. Tears were running down his face and sobs wracked him. He took the cigarette from my hand. His hands were shaking almost uncontrollably.

'Thanks chum. The wireless operator plugged in my intercom for me and connected my oxygen to the pilot's point. I just concentrated on flying.'

Bunny collapsed on his bed and wept. He was obviously not going to tell us more. Not till he was ready. And we were not going to rush him. We both felt that he would be better if he could talk it out of his system.

Brew shifted his huge frame in the only armchair of the hut. 'Could you see us at that point, Bunny?' Was it concern or curiousity in his voice?

'I didn't look. My shoulder was giving me hell. It was that bloody draughty and cold. I just wanted to fly the bloody thing and get home.'

Another great sob wracked his lanky frame. He drew deeply on his cigarette and choked on the smoke and sobs that welled up in his throat.

'I saw you first some time after the flak had stopped.' Another fit of coughing competed with his sobbing. 'You were in front and above me. I saw you, Robbie, but I daren't let go of anything to wave in case I couldn't get a hold again.' He looked at us both. 'I'll never forget the way you came back for me. Most awfully decent of you, you know. Really cheered me up. Just when I needed it, too.' He smiled weakly and looked more composed. 'I think perhaps we would have bailed out but for you coming back and helping us. I wanted to give up so many times on the way home. I was afraid to stay with the aircraft and I was afraid to bail out and leave those two. Oh, my God. I was so afraid.'

He turned his head to the pillow and wept as another wave of grief set him sobbing again. He lay like that for a minute or two, then sat up and faced us again.

'Funny the thoughts that go through one's mind. I can clearly recall I so wanted to get home, and so wanted to end it all.' His hands were shaking as he picked at a small scab on his knuckle.

Nothing was said for a few minutes. Bunny was wrapped in his own thoughts and I was recollecting the sight of the wounded Lancaster. I don't know what Brew was thinking, but he went to his bed space and returned with a bar of Canadian chocolate. He broke it into three and handed each of us a piece. We chewed away on it, respecting the silence that Bunny seemed to need.

Brew broke the silence at last. 'Well, Bunny. You couldn't have had a much worse trip. So, short of the big blade, things have got to get better for you.' He tossed a piece of tin foil into the coal bucket and continued. 'The worst thing that can happen to a crew is to have a run of lucky Ops first. They think that operational flying is a piece of cake and get over-confident. I reckon that has been the chop for more crews than bears thinking about. What do you reckon, little man?'

He was looking directly at me. I could not disagree. We had seen it happen all too often.

*   *   *

The three of us got along fine. Bunny had an old vintage Daimler. A two-seater with a dicky seat in the back. We would speed off together whenever we could. Sometimes, a pub crawl. Sometimes, to a film in town. And sometimes, just around the near country, scrounging eggs from the local farms. Sometimes, a combination of the three. And who was the one always in the open dicky seat? Who else but arse-end Charley. Me!

Night bombing was again the thing. Daylights seemed history. Bunny and his crew were doing reasonably well. However, some disturbing things emerged during the long conversations we had, huddled around the warmth of our stove in the cold winter nights of 1945.

It appeared that Bunny was in the habit of allowing his gunners to come onto the flight deck to get warm whenever they complained that their turrets were cold. Frankly, I was shocked at this revelation. Sure, a rear turret was colder than all charity. The mid-upper was only marginally better. But never did a gunner leave his turret just to get warm. Bunny seemed to think it was all right. I told him he was mad. He laughed, and told me that I panicked. I quietly trembled for his future.

Another daylight was sprung on us unexpectedly. We hadn't done one for sometime and had begun to think that Command had changed its tactics.

We were briefed for Bochum, a lesser city in the Ruhr Valley—called by many of us, Happy Valley. It was the usual briefing. High fighter cover. Pathfinder Force marking. All the old routine.

The ground defences were expected to be very heavy. The Ruhr always was. Orders were to fly straight and level all the way in, over the target, and all the way home. Lots of window to throw out to confuse the flak batteries.

Bunny was in 's'—SUGAR, just behind us as we taxied out from dispersal. We took off right on 0800 hours. I thought old 'E'—EASY would shake herself free of her rivets as we hung on our brakes with the four Merlins racing at full revs. Just when it seemed she would fall apart, we began to roll and were soon airborne.

's'—SUGAR was right behind us. He began his take off as we were retracting our undercarriage.

The airfield looked like an expensive toy. The planes, vehicles, buildings, fields and woodlands like so many models moving slowly across the face of the layout. I lost sight of *Sugar* as we circled the field to gain height. Soon there were so many aircraft that I was too busy watching out for those which may be on a collision course to worry about my hutmate.

It didn't take long to reach operational height. Then we were on course for the North Sea and the enemy coast. Hundreds of bombers stretched away in all directions. Each of them loaded with nearly ten tons of bomb to blast the industrial centre and railway yards of Bochum.

Friend Fritz sent up his welcome cards as we crossed the bomb line. The force flew through the flak as if it were not there. All but one. A Halifax spiralled to earth in flames to explode on the German side of the line. There was only one parachute.

'Who's the stupid son of a bitch weaving to port, Robbie?' It was Brew's voice. I had seen the errant Lancaster some minutes before and put it down to a new bird. It was too far away to see his letters.

'Your guess is as good as mine, old chum.'

'Watch the bastard. He could get us all in bother.'

'Will do.'

I watched it. Other Lancasters were steering clear of the erratic manoeuvres of the plane. That was all right, but it made a hole in the gaggle, and therefore a hole in the window cover. That made a hole in our defence system. Not desirable at all.

Holland was left behind as we crossed the Rhine. The flak began again as we entered the Third Reich. It was loose box barrage of mixed heavy and 88 mm dual purpose guns. Shells were bursting all around us. The hole in the gaggle seemed to come in for special treatment. We were on the edge of the hole and got a lot of the stuff meant for the delinquent Lancaster.

'Seven minutes to target, Brew. Course out of the target, three-five-zero degrees.' Sid's voice was calm and matter of fact. He couldn't see the flak coming our way but, like all of us, could feel it as it buffeted us around. Why did he sound so calm? I wanted to scream my fear.

'Target dead ahead, Brew.' Mel had just got the last syllable out when a heavy shell exploded close to our starboard wing. We lurched in the blast of it.

'Bloody hell! That blew a bloody great hole just above my bloody head. Bastard!' There was no mistaking our Australian wireless

106

operator's accent.

'Steady, Mac. Get back to the flare chute now!'

'Sorry, Brew. It scared me bloody fartless. Went right through the bloody kite. S'getting bloody dangerous. Going aft now.'

I don't know what the others felt. For myself, I liked Mac's humour. It WAS getting dangerous.

'Markers right ahead. Hold her as we go, Brew. We're spot on.'

Our big Canadian skipper would have his work cut out holding old *Easy* steady in this flak. It was all round. Thick, dirty, and dangerous.

The hard breathing of the only two crew with their mikes on came through the intercom.

'Steady! Steady! Bombs Gone!'

'E'—EASY lifted as she was released of her ten tons of high explosive. I watched as other Lancasters released their bombs. Cookies, five-hundred and one-thousand pounders fell like stones. Canisters of four-pound incendiaries scattered like firewood. A Lancaster astern was straddled with bombs from an aircraft above. I watched as incendiaries bounced off the fuselage. Scary!

'Bomb Doors Closed!'

Another shell burst beneath us, tilting the plane a few degrees. Brew brought it back to an even keel, his breathing like that of an old puffing steam engine as he laboured at the controls. I spotted the weaving Lancaster astern of us. The pilot was doing just about everything but loop his plane. Didn't he realize the danger he was to others?

'That stupid bastard's still weaving his guts out back here, Brew.'

'Thanks, Robbie. Watch the son of a bitch.'
'I am.'

And I did. The flak did not lessen as we left the target. I watched the offending Lancaster, and I watched the target. Smoke reached up thousands of feet in the air. Circular shock waves disturbed it as four-thousand pound cookies exploded among the fires. We were well clear of the target area and could still see the flash of bombs exploding in the unfortunate German city.

The course out of the target must have been an error by intelligence branch. We should have been free of flak by now, but the Germans still punched fire up at us. We must be over another defensive zone. Three aircraft in my sight were struggling to stay aloft. Two were on fire. The other had two engines feathered and a small wisp of smoke trailing from a third. Another shell burst close to us. Sid, our navigator, gave a cry.

'A bloody shell's just gone through me bloody table! Missed me by fuckin' inches. Went right through me bloody chart and out through the bloody roof. Thank Christ it didn't explode.'

'Wouldn't have known much about it, Sid.' Mac's dry sense of humour was like a safety valve.

And still the flak came up. The thick, oily tendrils of black obscenity appeared immune to the Lancaster slip streams as they flew through them. As the target receded, my old feeling of amazement that we could fly through such a labyrinth unscathed returned. Most of us, anyway.

I had been watching our weaving friend and noticed he was slowly converging on us. A Lancaster was on fire above and astern. One engine was feathered, and there was smoke pouring from another. Flame erupted from the wing, and it began to lose height, passing within yards of the weaving Lancaster. I was relieved to count seven parachutes bloom through the smoke of her death throes.

The flak lessened as the target was left behind. Our weaving companion steadied his erratic course and began to overtake us. When he was only about two hundred yards away and still converging, I thought it wise to pass the word to Brew in case avoiding action was called for.

Minutes later he passed gently across our stern, still gaining on us. As he approached our starboard beam I saw the letters. PH 's' stood out in the brilliant sunlight. I passed the news to Brew in a subdued voice. What the hell was

Bunny up to?

Mel reported more flak as we approached the bomb line again, and Brew wisely kept out of Bunny's sky when he started to weave again.

The flight over Holland and eventually England was without further incident. We landed in good order. It was not until we were in the mess that Bunny appeared.

He joined us at our table, and we stayed drinking an extra cup of tea while he ate. To say he was euphoric was an understatement. His whole being was alight with elation. His eyes brilliant in the grime of his sharp-featured face. His hands gesticulated. His voice an octave higher than normal. His verbiage bordered on the ridiculous as he recounted the past five hours.

Brew and I said nothing. There was no need. He wouldn't have heard anyway, so engrossed was he in telling of his part in the raid. There was no talk of his weaving, or of exposing crews and aircraft to collision.

Then, of course, there was the bombing run. What a brilliant spectacle! How perfect the marking! How accurate his bombing! And the flak. Wow! Surely no one had experienced it as bad as that before? But he had come through it all, hadn't he? Jeese! What an Op that was!

We had had enough. We were tired anyway, so we excused ourselves and headed for a shower and a lie down before dinner. Both of us feigned sleep as Bunny entered the hut. We heard him talking quietly to himself, and once or twice we heard him giggle in a childish sort of way. The creaking of his bed springs, then silence, told us he was doing what we all wanted to do: sleep.

Neither of us slept that evening. We were both worrying over the same problem. Bunny. And of course, neither of us solved it. He had gone over the edge. 'Flak Happy'. It took courage to report this, and we lacked it. To our sorrow as it turned out.

We didn't have the chance to talk with Bunny that night. A party developed in the mess. Though we joined in initially, and contributed enthusiastically to the early merriment, fatigue caught up with us. We crept off to Hut 21 and dived into bed.

Bunny was still asleep as we left for breakfast and a brief check on 'E'—EASY. At the flight office our flight commander told us that we had jumped the leave ladder and were to go on leave with effect 0800 hours that day.

We did a perfunctory check on our aircraft. More to say thank you and so long to our ground crew than to check the plane's operational readiness. I called at the armoury to see that our guns were fit to leave for a few days.

Armed with ration cards and railway warrants, we were soon on the noon bus for Lincoln and all points south. Brew and I spent a hectic two days in London, then headed for the quieter flesh pots of the Surrey countryside, where the ale was as sweet as the air. We were back at Wickenby in good time, almost glad of the security of Hut 21.

We didn't notice the empty bed at first. We assumed Bunny was out with his crew. Then we missed the gramophone that was usually on the table. The photographs were missing too. A glance at his bed confirmed our fears. His corner seemed lifeless.

Bunny's 's'—SUGAR had been one of two Lancasters missing from a raid on Essen two nights previously. Both the flak and the nightfighters had been exceptionally heavy. We wondered which had got Bunny. Perhaps he had allowed a gunner to come forward to get warm? Perhaps his erratic weaving had caused a collision? Perhaps. Would we ever know? Probably not. Bunny and his crew were Missing, Believed Killed.

*　　　*　　　*

Brew and I finished our tour. He returned to Canada while I stayed on at Wickenby. The European war finished in May 1945. Twelve Squadron went to Binbrook soon afterwards and settled into the luxurious pre-war quarters vacated by 460 RAAF Squadron.

We had only been there a few days when I heard a whoop from across the palatial floor of our new officers mess. It was Bunny.

Somehow, he had survived a mid-air collision and parachuted to the safety of a prisoner-of-war camp. He was the only survivor. He could not tell what had happened.

'It was suddenly pow! And I found myself in the air without old *Sugar*. I thought, "My God. Must pull the old ripcord!" I did, and found myself floating down to old terra firma. I was absolutely whacked when I got down. Got captured by an ancient German armed with a walking stick. Not a very dignified end to my war.'

There was no mention of his crew or the lead-up to the collision. No word of regret or remorse at the loss of six lives. There was nothing but a tense, euphoric Bunny.

But he was not the Bunny I had known. The spark had gone. He was empty. Sad. One of the casualties that didn't enter the statistics. I watched him go. A man as dead as any of the thousands who lost their lives in those years of political madness called War.

CHAPTER EIGHT

I SAY, SPRAY THAT AGAIN, OLD MAN

The Flying Control Tower of a war-time RAF airfield was just about the last place one would look for a Shakespearean actor. The tower at Royal Air Force Station, Wickenby could boast such a character during the dark days of winter, 1944–45.

In his way, a popular fellow, well-liked in the mess and a dedicated flying control officer. But not without some social reservations. He was very good at his job, and a reassuring voice as you entered the Wickenby Circuit, especially after a dicey do. His articulate, cultured voice over the air was like a shaft of light in a world of darkness. It was then that you felt you were Home.

At his age he was quite ancient by the standards of his aircrew audiences—for that is what we often felt ourselves to be. As I was saying, at his age he could well have avoided active service. But that was not his way.

He would often claim, 'One of me many regrets in life is I can't go where you chaps go night after night. Marvellous you are. All of you. Simply'—and here he was likely to shower you with a light spray of spittle—'bloody marvellous. Heroes, every man jack of you.'

Now, we had two fox masks hung over the fireplace. Ops-On was a miserable looking creature, with doleful eyes and a long face. The other—Ops-Off—was a much happier animal altogether. When we were flying someone—we never knew who—would throw a cap over Ops-Off's mask. When we were grounded, Ops-On wore the hat.

114

Most evenings when Ops-Off had his mask exposed, and conviviality was the order of the night, Flying Officer Derek Phipson—'spelt PH as in Twelve, don't you know'—could be seen embracing a pint of his usual and holding court, as we used to say. Generally with a group of new crews, expounding on some subject or other. Most likely the theatre, actors, or 'the play he would have had a lead in, but for ...', and so forth. Altogether, a likeable fellow. Twelve Squadron's aircraft letter began with PH.

To his credit, I don't think he missed an operation. He was always there to see us off, but more importantly, to get us down in one piece. But, socially, he was best taken in small doses.

I got to know Derek quite well in those days. For one reason or another, my spell with the 'Shiny Twelve' was longer than most. Part luck, part design by the hierarchy. So I was often called upon to be his 'Fall Guy' in theatrical parlance. After a couple of pints of good English ale Derek would wax poetic. He had been known to almost embrace a startled and innocent young flyer with, 'You're the salt of the earth, Old Man. I remember ...'—and he was off with his delightful woffle. Often spraying us all with a light sprinkling of beer droplets from his ale-sodden lips, reminiscent of a quick-firing shot-gun. He would look towards me at times and say, 'You remember,

Old Man ...' or 'But I've told you about him, haven't I?' And of course, he had. Many times. But with all his faults, when in the tower, sitting in front of that microphone, we were HIS men, flying HIS aeroplanes, in HIS war. The rest of the world could go to hell. Only his Wingco and the Groupy were allowed to gainsay this.

His Shakespearean talents erupted one night when a visiting concert party complained that one of their actors was ill and could not perform. 'Did we have some talent that could fill in for ten minutes?'

Derek was immediately into the breach.

'Wot's yer act?' asked the under-sized concert party manager.

'Just leave it to me, Old Chap. I know these fellows. The salt of the earth, every man-Jack of 'em.'

Perhaps it was unfortunate that Derek had not anticipated such an eventuality, for he had wined, if not dined, rather well in the mess prior to this headfirst plunge into RAF theatricals.

The airmen's mess was packed to the rafters. The air was dense with the fug of tobacco fumes and the smell of several hundred bodies in close proximity. The show opened with a display of scantily-clad chorus girls that brought howls and whistles from all ranks. The comic singer was a success too. As was the ribald comedian who left very little to the imagination.

Then it was Derek's turn. Perhaps he honestly thought the show needed a bit of culture after all the vulgarity of the 'legs and bums' and rather lewd jokes. Or perhaps it was the thought of a moment that could not be passed up. We will never know.

He emerged from the wings, heavily made up and costumed in a length of blackout curtain. With a look of pathos that had to be seen to be believed, he stood in a dramatic pose for a full minute. In about two seconds he had the attention of the whole audience. We didn't know what to expect. Comedy? Farce? Satire? What we didn't expect was:

'To be? Or not to be? . . .'

For a full quarter minute there was utter silence. I could hardly believe my eyes and ears. Then a chorus of catcalls and yells of abuse.

'Git art of it! Bring back the bloody birds!'

The curtain was hurriedly dropped. More catcalls and loud unflattering remarks.

The curtain was quickly raised again and three or four hundred sex-deprived airmen of all ranks were given a show of heel-kicking, bum-swaying, bosom-bouncing chorus girls. Anger and abuse changed in a moment to howls and catcalls of delight as two of us hurried to get Derek to the safety of his hut.

'I just don't understand it. Such wonderful prose and they don't want to hear it. I just don't understand?' And of course, he didn't. Probably, he never would.

It was quite late that night when I left him. A little drunk, and still recounting his near-burst into stardom with the 'Old Vic', or this or that repertory company. I was conscious that I could be flying tomorrow, and would need a good night's sleep. I left him sitting, still a little amazed at the lack of culture in the common man.

He was on duty and ready to go early the next morning. In answer to a quizzical look from me he exclaimed, 'The show must go on, Old Man. We must never weaken.'

And it did. Chemnitz in Eastern Germany was the target that night and Derek was there for the take off. And again for the landing. 'Grateful to Brylcream Easy. Angels three. Number five. Runway four. Over.' As reassuring as ever. We were home.

Some time later the squadron had been briefed for a daylight attack on Cologne with a take off time of 0800 hours. Some thirty aircraft from both Twelve and 626 Squadrons were involved. To ensure a quick take off, the thirty planes were lined up, nose to tail, on the perimeter track. There was little to fear from the Luftwaffe in those early days of 1945. Not in daylight anyway.

I was on the roof of the control tower to watch. I was always impressed at the precision and power of these huge aircraft as they defied gravity and soared into the air. The power that took a mass of metal, high explosive—and yes, blood, bone and tissue—thousands of feet into the air for a journey of hundreds of miles, never ceased to amaze me. Especially the take offs.

I watched PH 'C'—CHARLIE position himself for take off. The roar of the engines came to me as they reached maximum revolutions. I could almost feel the Lancaster shuddering and shaking as it tried to move against the wheel brakes. As the tail trembled and tried to lift, I saw the aircraft begin to roll forward. At that moment I was startled by the firing of a red signal flare just below. My eyes took in the whole scene. 'C'—CHARLIE cut back his engines. I ran for the parapet edge and looked over. Gesticulating arms were pointing towards the far end of the runway. There, loping down the centre, was a dot that appeared to be a dog. As I watched, other dog-like creatures appeared. Then a horseman. Then another. I heard a bellow of mortification from the depths of the control tower. Derek emerged and flew down the stairs and leapt on the running board of the crash tender.

'After them,' he screamed. The startled driver put the tender into gear and was moving as I clambered onto the opposite running board. Derek was beside himself with rage. 'How dare they! They must be mad!' he yelled. I heard his voice above the roar of the tender's engine.

The droplets from his lips were lost in the spray of puddles as we sped over the sodden grass. We were on the runway now and racing along at forty miles an hour. I looked across at Derek and laughed at the sight of his inflated cheeks and staring eyes until I realized that I must have looked equally odd. I could feel the wind filling my cheeks and bringing tears to my eyes.

We lost sight of the fox. But the hounds and the hunt were well in sight and veering off the concrete.

'After them!'

We cut in front of the pack with a swerve that almost sent Derek and I sprawling onto the soggy grass and skidded to a stop.

A figure in mud-splattered hunting-pink approached at a canter, his face an image of purple rage.

'By God! You could've killed one of me hounds!' he bellowed.

In the months that I had known Derek he had never but never been at a loss for words. But this nearly floored him. His face went a sort of puce colour. He began to boil from the tunic belt buckle up. I couldn't see the rest of him.

He recovered and drew himself to his full height—he looked quite impressive in his anger—and in a hardly audible voice said, 'How dare you, sir. How dare you.' As if finding a deep source of courage, he repeated it again. 'How dare you invade MY airfield and charge—yes, sir, charge—down MY runway. How dare you stop MY aircraft from taking off to fight MY war.'

By this time we had a gathering of about twenty horsemen and women milling around the fire tender. The hounds had been whipped in and were there too. I could see the Groupy's car coming down the runway at full speed. It splashed onto the grass and sped towards us.

'I say. I'm most awfully sorry. Didn't realize where we were. Had the bits between our teeth, you know. So sorry.' The Master of the Hunt, the gentleman in the mud-splattered hunting-pink looked shame-faced.

'Sorry be damned. Be off with you before I have you all clapped in irons.' Steady, Derek, I thought. That's over-doing it a bit. But I couldn't help smiling when he added as an afterthought, 'And take these clod-hopping yokels with you. And these flee-bitten hearth rugs you call hounds.'

A much mollified Master of the Hunt withdrew with the hounds at his heels just as the Groupy pulled up alongside.

'What the hell goes on, Phipson?'

'A bloody fox hunt and hounds on the runway, sir. But everything is under control. I'm terribly sorry, sir.'

'Very well. Best get back to control now and get these planes off the ground.'

Derek wiped his mouth with the back of his

hand and we both squeezed into the tender.

'Well this won't kill the Hun. Let's get on with the bloody war.' He sat back and wiped his mouth again.

Minutes later 'c'—CHARLIE was thundering down the runway and twenty-eight minutes later the last aircraft was airborne and circling the field to gain height.

'Nectar, me boy. Pure nectar,' exclaimed Derek.

We were standing, drinking mugs of hot, sweet tea and leaning on the window-sill of the control room, watching the Lancasters.

He placed his half-drunk mug on the table while he lit a cigarette. When it was going he smiled. 'We got 'em off in under one a minute. Good show, eh? Would have done better but for that bloody hunt. Put us twenty minutes behind schedule. Cheeky bastards.'

He was there when they came home and talked them all down. In the mess that evening, with his glass of 'Good English Ale', he told an interested audience of the incident, with no little embroidery.

'And there I was,' he laughed, 'superbly mounted on the crash tender. Charging over the green sward of Merrie England. Much like Richard the Third at Bosworth.' Only the new crews stood within range of the spray.

As a seventy-two hour stand down had been announced, it went on and on. It was not until the sound of the piano penetrated the corner of the mess, and Derek was down to an audience of one—me—that he exchanged prose for song and we joined the 'ops-types', old and new, in the ballads that have been sung by warriors the world over throughout the centuries.

During a short lull in the singing the Groupy asked our tipsy Derek, 'What happened to the fox, Phipson?'

'Got clean away, sir.'

'Splendid. Must have been a good omen. The target well pranged today and no aircraft lost.'

As Derek was about to embrace the Groupy and spray one of his lengthy monologues, the wily group captain withdrew discretely. He knew Derek.

The trusted old flying control officer took his demobilisation early. 'Must return to the boards, Old Friend. I have much to do, now that the dust of war has settled.'

We shook hands and I almost thrust him onto the bus for Lincoln before he could begin a long speech.

*   *   *

I never saw Derek again. I heard him on the BBC late in 1948 or '49 telling the story of a bomber squadron. I recognized some of the many characters. I knew it was Derek and that he was talking of the Shiny Twelve when he said, 'We led the field. So like the fox.'

123

It made me quite nostalgic. Years later I learned he was in a BBC soap opera. I was talking to an old Twelve buddy at a re-union, who repeated a story told by Derek. It seems that Derek was playing the part of a police sergeant in a serial and, during a break in shooting, he took a holiday in the west country. While having a usual in the local pub an old gaffer approached him with 'I know's you, dun' I?'

'Good,' replied Derek.

'Be you on the telly, then?'

'Oh, I'm in such and such,' replied Derek.

'Ar,' said the old gaffer, 'I do enjoy that show. But I can't stand the sight o' that bloody police sergeant bloke though.'

Dear old Derek. He hadn't changed.

The same buddy told me that he had died recently. Painlessly, I hope.

Derek Phipson never made stardom, but he'll always be a star of Twelve to me.

CHAPTER NINE

THE IMMORTALITY OF
KARL HEINRICH EHRENBURGER

The sun shone on the bride. As she stepped from the battered taxi at the church she made everything and everyone look and feel a little shabby. She was beautiful. Against the drab wartime scene, the shabby pre-war dress fashions made the wellwishers look like common sparrows in the presence of a Bird of Paradise. Only the sky, the trees and the sunshine could compete with her for sheer loveliness. Her father, Police Sergeant 'Dan' Wheeler escorted her through the lych-gate, up the few steps to the church and on to the west end of the short nave. Karl stood at the altar, waiting for her.

Karl Heinrich Ehrenburger was a Flying Officer (Navigator). Standing with him as best man and groomsman were his pilot, Flying Officer 'Eddy' Thomson, and his bombaimer, Flying Officer 'Johnny' Felgate. All were members of the Royal Canadian Air Force and, like me, were the crew of a Lancaster bomber stationed 'somewhere' in Lincolnshire.

I was there as a courtesy. A friend of the groom, and yes, of the bride too. I was present when they met and had watched their romance grow. It was really love at first sight for the pair of them.

Karl was a handsome fellow. He always looked good. Especially today. He was tall and fair, and looked, as his name hinted, Germanic. In truth, he was a German— German-born. His parents migrated to Canada from Pforzheim in Baden, Southern Germany, when Karl was only a few weeks old, in 1920. Karl knew no other country than Canada. He could speak only English. His parents were assimilated into Canadian life, not even teaching their son to speak his mother tongue. They were determined to bring their boy up as a Canadian in the country that had given them opportunities he would never had had in their native Germany. They wanted him to grow in an atmosphere of free speech, religion and thinking, away from a history of war and defeat and the turmoil created by it. Karl's father had considered anglicising their German name to Freeman, but rejected the idea, wanting his son to make up his own mind when he became a man. Upon coming of age Karl had refused to change his name.

'I was born Ehrenburger. It was good enough for father. It is good enough for me.' So Karl Ehrenburger he was. What's in a name anyway?

I was a Flying Officer, but a sub-human rear-gunner. Not even in the same air force, but friends all the same. We had been flying together for months now.

At the time of Karl's wedding we had completed fifteen operations over Germany. The autumn and late months of 1943 were not a good time to be flying. Nineteen-forty-four was no better. We had joined the squadron as the Battle of Berlin was drawing to a close. We only went to the 'big city' twice. That didn't upset us too much. Not going more often, I mean. We were badly shot up on both occasions. Once by flak over the target and the second time by a night-fighter on the way home. The Junkers-88 caught us with a burst of cannon fire before we were able to shoot it down. Fred Simpson, our Australian mid-upper gunner was killed, and 'Lofty' Leghorn, our Scottish flight engineer badly wounded. We had bad memories of Berlin. Bad dreams too, sometimes. It was my worst nightmare.

The organ struck up as Mary and her father began their long walk to the altar. 'Just plain Mary' was how she had introduced herself to us all then we first met her.

Karl was a fairly christian chap. A Lutheran back home in Saskatoon. None of us were church-goers. I was C of E—Christmas and Easter. Karl had talked the three of us into going to church in this tiny Yorkshire village near where we were stationed at the time.

It had been a lovely spring Sunday afternoon, I remember. We had cycled five miles to drink at the little pub. Karl saw the old Saxon church first and suggested we look inside. Personally I wasn't too keen. We had looked forward to a few beers but there was plenty of time before the pub opened. Karl was a nice bloke and the church was unusual, so what the hell?

We went from the church into the churchyard and were looking at the moss-covered tombstones. We were fascinated by the captions on the faded headpieces. Well, people began arriving for evensong and it was easier to go in with them than refuse Karl's pleading look.

The ancient cleric gave a good sermon and invited us all into the vestry for a cup of tea after the service. Karl wanted to go, so Eddy, Johnny and I tagged along. There were about thirty of us. Mostly ladies. The three of us felt a little out of place but Karl was perfectly at home.

We had nudged each other at the sight of the four girls sitting in a pew across from us. A few grins had evoked a shy smile or two. I thought that Karl had not even seen them, yet there he was with a cup of tea in one hand and a bun in the other, talking to one of them as if he had known her all his life.

It was Johnny's idea to join them. The girl's three friends came over and we were introduced all round. When it came to the dark haired girl talking to Karl, she looked at us with a twinkle in her eye.

'I'm Mary,' she said. 'Plain Mary.'

Plain? She was anything but plain. She was tall. As tall as Karl, and he was nearly six feet. She had what Lofty called a 'well-covered chassis'. Her hair was dark—nearly black— and long. She had blue eyes and rosy cheeks. What struck me at the time was that she had no make-up on. No lipstick. Nothing. She was beautiful.

We all walked the girls home and were invited into Mary's for a final cup of tea and to meet her parents. The girls were neighbours so it was no hardship to leave Karl with Mary and each walk one of the girls home.

On the bike ride back to the mess in the dark we all agreed that if church-going was like that then we would be regular attenders. And we were. For Karl and Mary, it was the beginning of their short courtship.

For the few weeks we were stationed on the training course we were able to attend that little church every Sunday. The five-mile cycle ride seemed short. The little pub in the village was never visited. It was a happy time. The families of the girls and the church congregation were kind and made us most welcome in their homes. The romance between Karl and Mary blossomed before our eyes, making we three feel privileged to be a little part of it.

The four of us were quite unhappy when it was time to move on. Our course had finished. We were posted to a squadron miles away to the south. Even to another county: Lincolnshire. Across the River Humber.

Karl bought a low-powered motor cycle and would travel to see Mary as often as operations allowed. When he wasn't visiting her they were telephoning, and there was a letter for him most days. We were all happy for him.

He never told Mary about the loss of Fred

and the wounding of Lofty. It was rather unfair, I thought. She really did not know what we were doing on the squadron, other than what she read in the newspapers. Apparently Karl hid from her the nightly horror that we shared.

I stood at the back of the church as they took their vows. I heard them plainly and joined in the blessing for them. I was the official photographer, with a borrowed camera and film scrounged from Photographic Section. The church was packed with relations, friends and well-wishers from the countryside—the Wheelers were a popular family in the county. As the organ struck up the Wedding March I positioned myself at the door to catch them as they came out.

It was a brilliant day. I clicked until I ran out of film. The reception was held in the little village pub. So you see, we did eventually have a drink there. Eddy, Johnny and I made ourselves scarce after the reception. The bridal couple did not want us hanging around. We caught the bus to York and sampled the hostelries in the old city for a few days until it was time to return to the squadron.

Surprise! Karl was there before us. He and Mary had returned from their honeymoon early and had spent a day seeking out rooms in the neighbouring village. They set up house there and we were frequent visitors. Often for meals and frequently just to see them and enjoy their company.

The weeks turned into months. One operation followed another. Twenty-nine, and no real bother since the last Berlin Op. A few holes in the old Lancaster and lots of frights. But that was all. Our luck had been good.

*   *   *

It was a fine winter's day. The battle order was out and we were flying. Briefing 1700 hours. We had done our checks. Our aircraft was fueled and bombed up. There was nothing unusual in the petrol and bomb loads to tell us that it was anything but a usual prang. As we went to the mess for lunch we watched Karl's little motor cycle disappear in a cloud of blue smoke. We knew he would be back well before briefing. He always was.

We three bachelors went to our hut after lunch for an hour or two's sleep. It could be a long night ahead.

We were in the mess having a last cup of coffee after our operational meal when Karl arrived and we all walked over to the briefing room. There was a crowd around the map on the raised dais when we got there.

'No bloody hurry. We'll know the target soon enough. No good worrying too early.' Eddy's laconic remark set us at ease. He was right, of course. This was to be our last operation. The one we had looked forward to for months. The one we were most afraid of now.

The crowd thinned around the map. We all looked at the red tape that marked the route, following the zigzag across the map of Europe to the large-headed yellow pin that marked the target.

None of us spoke. Words failed us. I looked at Karl and saw he had turned a little pale. There, under the point of the pin, was Pforzheim.

'Shit!' The oath exploded from Eddy. 'Of all the bloody targets to have for a last op. It had to be bloody Pforzheim.'

Karl looked at the map. 'Looks like a good route in and out. No bad areas to shoot us up. I reckon night-fighters will be the biggest problem.' He was talking fast to cover his distress. We knew he still had relatives in Pforzheim.

We were a silent group that took our seats. The three NCO crewmembers did not know what we were thinking. Why should they? They were not as close as us. The four of us had spent long hours in argument and discussion over the months together, talking of ourselves—our hopes—our plans for the future.

The plans for the world we would make from the debacle of the nineteen-forties. Karl, I remember, wanted to be a teacher. Eddy, an architect. Johnny had ambitions to be a dentist. And myself, a forester. There seemed such a permanence in the word. Forester. So creative. The things we would do. The crusade we would launch against corruption and greed. Heady stuff for our young minds. We also talked of our pasts.

I missed most of what the Wingco said. I was too busy planning to button-hole him after the briefing to allow Karl to stand-down for this one.

The briefing followed the usual pattern of navigational problems, tactics and the rest of the patter. It broke up and the crews dispersed to gather their flying gear and get out to the aircraft. Karl went off to the nav section to get his charts and instruments. We three sauntered over to the Wingco.

'May we have a private word with you, Sir?'

'Hello, chaps. What's the problem?'

We spent ten minutes telling him of Karl's parentage and his place of birth.

'Damn! Damn bad luck, what? Get him to my office at once and we'll see what we can do.'

The four of us were in the Old Man's office in ten minutes. The Wingco was sitting behind his desk.

'I know the circumstances, Karl, and I am standing you down.' His words had a finality about them.

'Please don't. Sir. We have diced together throughout the tour. Don't break us up. Besides, it will mean me going as a spare bod with another crew to finish my tour.'

There was some discussion on both sides. We said we would do an extra trip to take him on his last. Karl was adamant. He was going.

'I told my wife it was my last one, Sir. I don't want her to have to worry after tonight. You see, Sir, she is going to have a baby.'

There was nothing any of us could say to that. The Wingco sighed and raised his hands helplessly. We were committed. Destined to fly to Pforzheim.

'Good luck then, chaps. It's very plucky of you, Karl.' The squadron commander reached across and shook Karl's hand.

We were late out to our aircraft. The run-up and equipment checks were hurried through and we were ready in time for our scheduled take off. We taxied out and took our turn for the green light. The engines were opened full and we were away.

The night was dark. The met had forecast no moon and full cloud over the target. The Pathfinders would be using the *Wanganwi* sky markers. The route in was no problem. A little flak as we got too close to Rotterdam on the way in, but it was very inaccurate. We made a feint at Frankfurt and then went straight for Pforzheim.

The weather-man was right. The target was covered with cloud. We were in the first wave and a few seconds early. The PFF markers were late, so we orbited and came in again. A shower of brilliant white sky markers lit up the clouds as we levelled out on the approach. The flak was erratic but intense. Shells were bursting at our height and all around us. Searchlights played on the cloud ceiling and lit up the clouds beneath us. It was as light as day. A huge white tablecloth with beetle-like bombers crawling over it. I saw a Lancaster get a direct hit from a shell and explode. A four-engined Halifax way down on our starboard was streaming smoke.

I called to the mid-upper. 'A good night for cat's eye fighters. Keep an eye open above us!'

Ronny was a new bird. A young sergeant—only a schoolboy really. It was his second op. We had never had a permanent replacement for Fred.

A cluster of brilliant green and red markers cascaded smack in the middle of the whites. Bang on. Our orders were to sight on the centre of the whites.

Eddy bought the Lancaster onto the bombing run. He had just levelled out when Johnny gave the order.

'Bomb Doors Open!'

Almost immediately a flak shell burst underneath us. Close.

'My God! Get rid of those bloody bombs!' My thoughts willed Johnny to hurry. But Johnny never hurried on the bombing run.

'What's the point of going through all hell to get there, hell while you are there, hell again to get home, and not make sure your bombs go where they will hurt most?'

Johnny's philosophy was right, of course, but oh, the agony of waiting to feel that blessed lift.

'Left left!' Johnny's orders to his pilot a phlegmatic calm.

How he could sound so calm was always a mystery to me. I always wanted to scream my fear. To compensate for this I sang the craziest songs sometimes. Once I remember singing *This is a lovely way to spend an evening*. Over the target! With flak bursting all round me. I must have been mad.

'Steady now. Steady. Steady. Bombs Gone!'

'Photo Flash Gone, Eddy.' This latter call from our wireless operator at the flare chute.

The old Lancaster seemed to feel lighter when the bombs and the photo flash had gone. I felt lighter too. What a relief to be rid of all that high explosive.

I saw movement down on the starboard quarter. A Lancaster was being fired on by a Focke-Wulf 190 'cat's eye' fighter. There was no answering fire from the two turrets. The German was only about two hundred yards from me and silhouetted against the brilliance of the target. He seemed unaware of our presence.

'Corkscrew starboard. Go!' My call for the combat manoeuvre coincided with my firing the four Brownings into the fighter. I held onto the triggers and saw the tracer bullets hose into

136

the cockpit area. As we broke away for a climb to port, the FW exploded in mid-air. The Lancaster was spiralling down, with smoke pouring from it.

'Watch out port up. He's probably got a chum.' My message was meant for the mid-upper gunner and the wireless operator who would be watching from the astrodome.

'Dive port!'

Eddy threw the Lancaster over on its wing. Tracer flew over my head from the mid-upper guns.

The nineteen-year-old gunner was pounding bullets into another FW diving onto us. We must have been a good target, silhouetted as we were against the lit-up cloud base.

Eddy pulled the bomber up onto a climbing turn to starboard as a hail of cannon-shell struck us. I felt the 'Crump!' and jar of them as they ripped into us. I didn't need to hear Ronny's scream to know we had been hit. The Lancaster faltered for a second before it climbed. The Focke-Wulf passed before my vision. It was close and trying to follow us round. So close that in the light from the fires and searchlights I saw the pock-marks of the mid-upper's bullets in the fuselage. The black cross on the side of the German plane seemed to beckon me. I pressed my triggers and saw my tracer strike it. I kept my fingers flexed on the triggers. The note of the four Brownings changed as one gun jammed. I kept firing. The fighter hung on. His nose was pointing directly at me. The blunt nose of the radial engine seemed monstrous; the yellow-painted spinner of the propeller staring straight at me like a jaundiced eye. And still I fired into it, willing it to go away and leave me with my fear. Another gun jammed. The remaining two glowed a dull red but kept pouring fire into the enemy. I couldn't miss. But neither could he!

I was raving. Cursing the pilot for not dying. Willing the fighter to either fall out of the sky or break away. We were at the top of our climb. Eddy was putting our kite into a dive. Another burst of cannonfire came at us. It struck the tailplane close to me. I had one gun left. The barrel glowed red.

As we went into our dive I saw the Focke-Wulf break away. There was flame and smoke coming from its engine.

'Resume Course. Go!'

I was sobbing into my oxygen mask. Tears were cold on my cheeks and I was shaking. Whether from fear, relief or reaction I didn't know. I hadn't time to consider it. I knew I was alone back here. There was the whole Luftwaffe out there looking for me and hungry for a kill. I saw the enemy plane disappear through the cloud. I watched the spot where it had gone and saw a flash from beneath the cloud. Had it crashed? I would never know.

I didn't need to be told Ronny was dead. I cleared my guns and checked my ammunition-feed mechanism. My intercom mike was still on and I found I was still raving between my sobs. My thumb moved and I switched the mike off.

'You OK, Robbie?' Eddy's voice cut through the mists of fear and anger. His breathing, hard from the exertions of the last minutes. Only minutes? We had lived a lifetime.

'Yes.' It was all I could say. I couldn't trust my voice to say more. I took a minute to get myself and my guns into order. 'How are you up there? Were we hit bad?'

'Ronny and Alex have had it and Karl is in a bad way. Lofty's caught a packet in the legs and is out cold. Johnny is fixing the guys up. What does the kite look like from your end?'

I swung my turret to beam and peered the length of the fuselage. The target was behind us now and the light was poorer, but even so I could see light through large holes where none should be. The cannon shells to the tail had missed the elevators.

'It looks a bloody mess. I dare not leave the turret for a closer look. What d'you reckon?' I was searching the sky again. We still had a long way to go.

'It feels OK. All A-OK this end. You sure you're OK?'

'Fine.' It was not too much of an exaggeration.

'I'll send Johnny back for a check as soon as

he's finished looking after the guys. OK?'

'OK, Eddy. And thanks.'

'Thank you, Robbie.'

The night got dark again. The intercom was silent. I was cold, frightened and lonely. Alone. The only pair of eyes. And God only knew what I would see. Or not see. Maybe, never see again?

I saw three bombers shot down on the way home. Night-fighters pursued us even into the runway funnels at home base. Intruders, that caught the bomber silhouetted against the runway lights with their wheels down, ready to land. 'F'—FOX was caught at our base just before we arrived. We saw it burning in the funnel mouth as we made our approach.

'Caught like a bishop with his britches down in the actress's bedroom,' was the way a pilot described it at interrogation.

Flying control had warned us of bandits and normally we would have remained clear of the airfield until it was clear of the enemy. But we had wounded aboard. Johnny choked on a sob when I asked how Karl was. He didn't tell me. He didn't have to.

The blood waggon followed us to our dispersal. I sat in my turret, letting the fatigue and tension ease from my body. Wanting to see Karl and Lofty, but afraid of what I might see. I heard the ambulance drive away. Johnny knocked on my doors. I opened them and clambered out, passing him. Eddy came back down the fuselage after looking at our young mid-upper gunner, still hanging there in his turret, the fuselage slippery with his blood. We met at the rear door and fell into each other's arms. It was still dark. I cannot speak for the others, but I wept.

We were standing there when our cockney sergeant fitter poked his head into the kite.

'You blokes OK? 'Ad a dicey do, I 'ear?'

His face was white in the pre-dawn darkness. The tinkling of the engines as they cooled was loud in the silence.

'We're OK, Spud. Don't let your fellars in here until the blood waggon has been again.'

'Bad as that, is it? Bit of a mess, are they? Poor sods.'

'Yeah. Mid-upper gunner and the wireless op.'

'Bowf of 'em? Poor buggers. S'only a kid, ain't 'e? Mid-upper, I mean. You sure you're awl right?'

'Yeah. Sure, we're fine.'

And we were. We were alive. Tired, dirty, and still shaken. But alive. Mostly, we were afraid. Afraid for Karl, our personal fears of the last hours forgotten for the time being.

We clambered down the ladder as the crew bus rolled up and were driven to interrogation.

We hardly spoke. The meal got cold in front of us. The cigarettes burned unheeded between our fingers. Our thoughts were with those of our absent crew. Especially Karl. Was he all

141

right? Would he live? Who would tell Mary?

The Wingco came in as we sat facing each other. The coffee in our cups was cold.

'Hello chaps. What can I say?' He was almost as shocked and upset as we were, and he had this sort of thing nearly every night. Some wife or mother to tell that her man had not returned. 'Missing, Believed Killed.' It was a very final statement.

'When you are ready, I have arranged for a vehicle to take you to see his wife. Mary, isn't it? Tell her how sorry I am. We all are. And that I will see her when she comes to visit her husband. She may come when she likes. As often as she likes. I'll take the responsibility.'

He stood up to leave. 'Don't take it too hard. You all put up a marvellous show. The squadron is proud of you. All of you.'

We washed the filth of the flight off us and a WAAF driver drove us to the large Victorian house in the village where Mary lived.

Mary met us at the door.

'It's Karl, isn't it? Is he dead?'

'No, Mary. But he's pretty sick.' Somehow, Eddy took a natural lead in things. That's why he was the skipper, I suppose.

'When can I see him?'

'The Wingco said anytime, but I would wait for a while. Let the Doc fix him up first.'

It was Johnny who spoke. I felt so ashamed. So tongue-tied. So impotent. There was so much I felt, yet my mind could not find the words. I suddenly realised I loved this girl—not romantic love, but the love I would have given the sister I never had. I wanted to take all the pain from her and bear it myself. Why could it not have been me who was wounded and not Karl? Mary seemed to understand. I felt her eyes on me. I looked up. She smiled a tearful smile at me.

'Come in, Robbie. All of you. Come in and pray with me. For Karl and the others.'

None of us were worshippers, but the four of us knelt unashamedly and Mary led us in prayer for the lives of the wounded and the souls of the dead that night. Friend and foe. She had such a strength, and part of it passed into us.

We were in the mess two days later. Mary had been at the station sick-quarters all that time, sleeping in a special room the Wingco had arranged. Karl was too sick to move. His future was bleak.

He died a few days later. He had regained consciousness long enough to speak briefly to Mary. We never discovered what he said and we didn't ask. She was dry-eyed when we saw her walk out of the ward. As she was at the graveside at the little church where they had met and married.

*   *   *

Little Karl was born on 6 June 1944. The allied

armies invaded Hitler's Europe as if to celebrate. Eddy, Johnny and I were flying together over the Normandy beaches for both events. We all stood in as godfathers for little Karl.

The three of us finished our second tour and the long hard war came to an end. Eddy and Johnny returned to Canada and I went to university to study forestry. Mary and the baby lived with her parents in Yorkshire. Life went on in the dreary years of the late forties' rationing.

I was working in the Forest of Dean as a junior forestry officer when I received a letter from Eddy. He was coming to England and was going to marry Mary. It seems the two of them had been courting by mail for years. He had proposed marriage by mail. And she accepted by mail. The wedding was set for Easter Saturday. Two weeks away. I had to be there. It was an order.

My reply telegram read, 'REAR-GUNNER TO CAPTAIN. WILCO. OVER AND OUT'.

We all met in London: Mary, Eddy, Johnny and myself. And of course, our godson, Karl. The three of us had got a little drunk the night before. Not as a traditional thing, but because we had so much to talk about. Karl came in for a lot of mention. There was no embarrassment about Eddy marrying Mary. Johnny and I could not have been happier for them. And little Karl would have a father who loved him.

Mary and Eddy were married at a church in London. It was not the same as in Yorkshire but Mary looked as beautiful as she had all those years before. Little Karl looked important as her page boy.

I was the photographer again and clicked away with a camera I had picked up in Germany during my last months in the RAF. My eyes misted as I remembered.

Johnny and I saw them off at London airport for Canada. I was handling the tickets and passports. I opened little Karl's and saw the name: Karl Heinrich Ehrenburger.

*   *   *

The years have been good to all of us. Johnny married years ago and lives in Edmonton, Canada. He became a doctor, not a dentist. He and his wife, Joyce, live not too far from Eddy, Mary, and their family of four sons. They have all been to Western Australia where I have lived since my retirement.

I have been to Canada and visited them all. The last time was to my godson's wedding. Karl and his young American wife live in California. In a letter recently I learned of the birth of their son. Karl Heinrich Ehrenburger, the Third.

The world is not quite as we planned it in our youth. Things have changed, mostly, I believe, for the better. I am sure that Karl our navigator would have approved of most of the changes. He certainly would have been pleased at the immortality of his name. Karl Heinrich Ehrenburger has quite a ring to it.

CHAPTER TEN

AND THE DRINKS WERE ON KIWI

'Remember. Don't be fooled. The Hun only knows what you tell him. Number. Rank. And name. That's all.' Smithy's eyes tried to penetrate the thick fug of the crowded Nissen hut, euphemistically called Twelve Squadron Briefing Room. The room was packed to almost suffocating point with damp aircrew. The weather had clamped and all aircraft were grounded. Water fell from the low clouds in a thick soup-like mist. The whole of eastern England dripped under a steady fall of light rain. The young men of his audience were smoking a mixed bag of cigarettes, and tobacco from extravagant-looking pipes. The dense fumes mixed with the odour of damp clothes, muddy boots, hot breath and steaming bodies of one hundred and fifty young aircrew. The flying personnel of the 'Shiny Twelve'— Number Twelve Squadron, RAF Bomber Command.

Smithy,—Flight Lieutenant Smith, MC,— was a wiry little Scot of late middle age. He was the intelligence officer of Twelve Squadron and had just concluded a lecture on the latest German ruse for dealing with shot-down allied aircrew who had been wounded or shocked: thoroughly tranquilizing them so that they recovered between the white sheets of a hospital. A German hospital. A hospital where the nurses and doctors spoke faultless English.

The airman would recover his senses and look bleary-eyed into the eyes of an 'English' nurse who would extract all the relevant information. Squadron. Target. Location. Type of aircraft. And much more before the innocent flier was fully awake.

The Scot pulled a battered briar from his tunic pocket and, as he rammed tobacco into the charred bowl, cast his eyes around the room. They were a very mixed group of young men. Smithy loved them all. And they loved him. The white and blue ribbon of the military cross and the Royal Flying Corps pilot's brevette gave him the status of a veteran. Albeit a war ago. His limp proclaimed a wound in action and set him on a par with his young audience. His experience and understanding endeared him to fliers. His huge repertoire of bawdy ballads ensured him a place around the piano at mess parties, where he would out-sing and out-drink men half his age.

He placed the pipe in his mouth, struck a

match and lit it before asking: 'Any questions?' He did not expect an answer. He knew that with the aircraft grounded the young men had only one thought. The flesh-pots of Lincoln. 'Thank you, Wing Commander.'

The squadron commander trod out his ubiquitous Player's cigarette under a muddy boot and stood facing the crews.

'Stand down for tonight, chaps. The met promise a fine night for tomorrow so we may be dicing. Everyone report to their flights and sections by 0830 hours tomorrow. And please, no thickheads! Dismiss!'

There was much good-humoured jostling as the crews fought their way out into the dripping fresh air and onto the pot-holed roadway that led to the sergeants' and officers' messes.

Flying Officer 'Kiwi' Foldworth and crew burst onto the puddled road.

'Hey, Kiwi!'

The New Zealander took his arm from the headlock he had on his rear-gunner and went over to his flight commander.

'Yeah, Poppa?'

'Get your chaps over to the orderly room for their leave passes. You are all on leave from 0800 tomorrow. With this weather clamp, you may as well go today. Shove off then.'

'Gee. Thanks Poppa. You beaut.' He doubled over to his crew with the good news.

Squadron Leader 'Poppa' Huggins, now

commander of B-Flight watched the seven youngsters run through the dripping trees along the forbidden short-cut to the squadron orderly room. He was about to call a protest, but didn't. They were only young, and weren't they excited about their leave? He smiled grimly as he thought of the crew that should be going on leave.

'Missing. Believed Killed' from last night's operation over Hamburg. He pulled the collar of his raincoat tighter and made for the mess and a warming drink before he composed his letters to the next of kin. 'Damn the bloody war,' he thought, as he tramped through the puddles and rain after the airmen.

Kiwi was on the noon bus for Lincoln and the train to York via Doncaster. He had sent a telegram to his aunt and uncle at their farm near Selby to say he would accept their invitation to spend a leave with them. He had stayed there once, before joining Twelve, and had enjoyed the peace of the countryside.

His uncle Robert was the only member of the family to have ever left New Zealand. Uncle Bob had been an ANZAC when he had met his wife while on leave from France in 1917. She was an only child and when her father died during the influenza epidemic of 1919 it seemed natural for his son-in-law to stay and run the family farm.

The crew had had time for a quick drink before catching their trains. The one to

Doncaster was late, and later still when it reached its destination. So late he missed the York train.

It was still raining as he made for an old watering hole in the Yorkshire town. The Daneham Hotel. He was no stranger to the town or the bar. It had been a favourite of his when he was training at the nearby airfield. The elderly receptionist remembered him and gave him a room on the first floor. 'Overlooking the 'igh street and the park. Nicer than at the back looking at the gas works.'

Kiwi smiled at the sound of her Yorkshire accent. He threw his valise onto the bed and hurried to the bar.

Now Kiwi was by inclination and tradition a whisky drinker. A skill he had acquired from his maternal grandfather who had lived with them in the South Island. The old man was a McKenzie and hailed from a croft on the rocky cliffs of Caithness. He had gone to New Zealand from South Africa where, as a mere teenager, he had fought the Boers in the Battle of Majuba in 1881. As a young man he had carved out a small dairy farm from virgin forest. His only daughter had married an ANZAC who had been wounded at Gallipoli. The army found him 'Unfit for Active Service' so the two of them settled on the farm as well. All had lived happily as an extended family. Kiwi was born in 1920, an only child.

Grandfather and grandson were very close.

The old man's wisdom had taught Kiwi many things. One was a taste for good whisky; another was to drink it in moderation. Kiwi did this most times, to the extent that during periods of flying he never touched it. Sometimes for weeks at a time. But leaves were different.

There was no one in the bar except the barmaid. Kiwi never drank alone.

'Ave a grog?'

'Ta. Don't mind if I do. Wot'll it be then?'

'Scotch. With water. What about you?'

'I'll have a port and lemon. Ta.'

She poured the drinks and eyed the young New Zealander coyly. She was over-weight and a Henna red-head. Not Kiwi's type of girl and he was beginning to wish he had not been so friendly. He was saved from an embarrassment by the door opening to a Royal Navy lieutenant. Kiwi's relief was audible.

'My shout, cobber. What'll it be? I'm on leave and celebrating.'

The pair made their introductions and drank together. They were joined later by two RAF officers and a flight sergeant. One round of drinks followed another, until they were all quite tipsy. The barmaid called 'Time!' and the four visitors staggered out into the night. Kiwi staggered up the stairs to his room.

He reached the door by taking four steps forward and one back. This surprised him. Surprised too when the keyhole kept moving.

151

Having captured it, the key wouldn't go into the lock. Finally succeeding, he flung the door open with a victorious flourish and fell into the room.

He struggled across the floor to pull the blackout curtains closed, but changed his mind. With a crash he opened the window. The rain had stopped and the moon bounced around the clouds alarmingly.

*   *   *

The flak was intense box barrage. Flashes of heavy shells lit the sky momentarily and revealed black, oily puffs from the 88 mm flashless shells. Their elongated shapes took on the figures of obscene gargoyles, standing grotesquely immune to the slip-streams of the Lancasters flying through them. Searchlights reached out like giant claws. The crash of the shell that demolished their wing shook the whole plane. Flames burst from the two starboard engines. The scream from the mid-upper gunner pierced his eardrums.

The flight engineer fought the extinguisher switches. It was no good. The engines were a mass of flame. Smoke was coming from behind him as he sat at the controls. The Lancaster began to dip a wing. He was going into a spin. They would have to bail out.

'Jump, for Christ's sake I can't hold the bloody thing!'

He felt the draught as the bombaimer jettisoned the forward escape hatch. The flight engineer passed him with his parachute clipped on. He was followed by the navigator. The wireless operator came next and Kiwi screamed that his flying jacket was on fire. There was no response.

'Why don't you say goodbye!' he called to the disappearing figures. They looked at him as if they had heard. But they were the faces of his mother and father.

His screams unheard amidst the thunder of shell bursts. Flames, furnace-hot. Long, orange-red barbed tongues reaching like talons to devour him. With a super-human effort, he was out of his seat and through the hatch.

The night air was cold. He saw the moon below him? The ripcord was in his hand. He pulled it, and the moon exploded before his eyes.

*　　　*　　　*

Smell. That was the first thing he became aware of. The smell of Dettol and floor polish. Then, cheap perfume. His eyelids felt as if they were made of lead, but he forced them open. He found himself looking into a pair of blue eyes. Female eyes? Nurse? He tried to think but the pain in his head made it too much trouble. He tried again. This time the eyes focussed better but the pain was worse. He gave up.

'Awake at last, are we?' Her accent was Yorkshire. Rather pleasant. Not broad. 'How d'you feel now, then?'

Kiwi struggled to move but the lights before his eyes were too painful.

'Keep thee sen still while I get the doctor.' The smell of perfume went away and Kiwi lay trying to orientate himself.

'Well, old man, you seem to have had a heavy night. There are no bones broken and we will have you out of here in no time.' English voice? So was the nurse's?

'Now, if you will just tell me where you are from. Squadron. And that sort of thing. We'll just let your people know you are in good hands.'

Memories came flooding back. 'These bloody Germans!' The thought hit him like a thunder clap.

'Name, rank and number. That's all you have to tell them.' Smithy's words came flooding into his head.

Forty-eight hours later, Smithy was at his bedside.

'What a bother you ha' been, young Kiwi!'

It took the sight of the old intelligence officer to convince him that what they had been telling him was true.

Apparently, he had fallen from the first floor window of The Daneham and had been brought to the Royal Doncaster Infirmary.

154

By the time his concussion had cleared, he had only time to say 'hello' to his aunt and uncle and return to the squadron. There was much laughter as Kiwi's story was told and retold. When he entered the officer's mess the bell was rung. And the drinks were on Kiwi.

*   *   *

Flying Officer Foldworth and crew finished their tour of thirty operations and were posted to various training units. Kiwi finally managed to get some leave at his uncle's farm.

The rabbits were particularly good that year and Kiwi spent much of the time with a shotgun, bagging some for the pot as it were.

It was the fence that did it. Or the loaded shotgun. The coroner couldn't be sure which. But the inquest returned a verdict of 'Death by Misadventure'. Apparently Kiwi had been climbing through a fence with a loaded shot gun. The gun had gone off, accidentally I presume.

Kiwi was buried in the tiny churchyard of Bubwith. It's a tiny village near Selby in Yorkshire.

His grieving parents attended an investiture at Government House in Auckland to collect his Distinguished Flying Cross. His grandfather contented himself by walking through the native forest the two of them had visited so often and sitting under their favourite tree. And drinking a dram or two to his favourite grandson. Kiwi.

POSTSCRIPT

I finished another tour. I had fifty-five operations under my belt. It had been a good tour. They were a first class bunch of fellows. All NCOs. It was probably because of that that we were so happy. We flew together, lived in the same mess, slept in the same hut. We drank together and played together. One memorable night we nearly died together. Everything we had, we shared. Even girlfriends, sometimes. I was sorry when we split up to go to the various training units for a rest.

I hated the training units. Most of the instructors were aircrew but worked at avoiding flying. Especially when you would be shot at. I was scared too but Monty's words remained in my mind: 'If we must be wretched air-gunners, we may as well be good ones.' To Monty, being a good one meant getting on with the job we were paid for.

I chummed up with an NCO pupil crew of Australians. We would gather in the sergeant's mess at the OTU and spend hours talking and laughing together. I believe that with them, I regained my joy of life that I had lost after losing Monty and leaving Bonzo's mob and later, Eddie & Co.

Their rear-gunner contracted an ear infection that grounded him permanently.

Sergeant John Christensen—pilot—and crew were without a rear-gunner. I saw my chief instructor and, as my minimum six months' rest had expired two months ago, I was assigned as reargunner to the Australian crew. The only Pom amongst six Aussies.

Three months later I was back at Binbrook with 460 (Lancaster) Squadron, Royal Australian Air Force. With 460 we hit the Ruhr, Hamburg, Steetin, Konigsberg, Turin, Milan, Genoa, Pheenamunde and Berlin. Several times. We were shot at, crash landed, caught fire and nearly had to bail out. We claimed two night-fighters shot down but happily finished the tour without a drop of Australian blood being spilt.

The English blood—my own—was spilt in the English blackout. We had dined rather well at The Marquis of Granby—one of the only two pubs in Binbrook village. I ran into a wall when returning from the toilets on a dark night and received a nose bleed and a severe ribbing from the boys.

Sadly, we had to split up again. I was back on an OTU doing the instructor grind. I was quite senior now, an officer. I had collected a medal or two and, though I hardly carried myself with pride, I believe I had confidence in myself. I was under no delusion. I had been lucky—and lucky with my crews. Above all, I had been afraid. Very afraid. It engendered a survival capability. I had an ability to anticipate problems and planned to circumvent them. Experience, I suppose.

* * *

May 1945. My third tour, back with Twelve Squadron, and Hitler decided he had had enough. It was a relief. The officer's mess on VE Day was a riot. I got on my bicycle and rode for miles. I had been flying for five years and had lost many friends, not the least of whom were Fred and Monty. They were the first—the ones who had formed me, so to speak. I felt, as the mess developed into an orgy of celebration, that I wanted to be with them.

* * *

1949. My parents had been killed by a German rocket in 1944. There was nothing to keep me in England now. I had been accepted as a migrant to Australia. But there was one last thing I must do before I left. I had to see Monty's people.

I caught the train for Inverness. I had corresponded with the 'Brig' and told him of Monty's wish that I should see his people. The old general invited me to stay.

It was a more comfortable ride north this time, even in the third class carriage. I was able to catch the Stromeferry train with no waiting. Again, the highlands fascinated me. The names

159

of the small stations brought back memories. The ferry trip to the northern shore was pleasant and I caught the local bus to Kishorn. The MacNess residence was another two miles up the Glen. I passed the wee kirk and stopped to rest—as much to enjoy the view as to get my wind—before the last half-mile climb.

I looked up towards the house. An entourage was coming down the narrow road. I stood transfixed. As it got closer I saw it was a funeral procession. The same cart as Monty had been on, pulled by the same two Clydesdales. The Union Jack and the cap, sword and decorations of a major general were on the coffin. I did not need to be told it was the 'Brig'.

I followed the dozen mourners back to the little kirk and stood as the service was read. Monty's father was laid to rest beside his wife and son.

I stayed the night at the same little hotel and got drunk with the officer in charge of the firing party. The landlord recognized me and thought I was there for the old man's funeral. I didn't tell him different. He told me the 'Brig' had collapsed with a heart attack out on the moors. They found him next day.

My journey south—far south—was to begin a new life. A life with new friends. My ship called at Colombo and I had a happier meeting with 'The Old Fellar'—Mr and Mrs Cotton. I answered all their questions about Fred. It was a Sunday, so we attended the little church in the sunny hills above the city. The plaque on the wall read:

Sergeant Sinclare Cotton, RAFVR
Killed in Action over Germany
Born 1921—Died 1941

Dear God. How young we all were.

SOUTH LANARKSHIRE LIBRARIES

HOUSEBOUND SERVICE

R920015	R920	
R920125	44 330	
R920071	203 45	
	95 183	
	125	
	249 77	
	218 10	
	292	
	335	
	011	